Church Administration

Church Administration

A Devotional and Motivational Guide

CLIFFORD MUSHISHI

RESOURCE *Publications* • Eugene, Oregon

CHURCH ADMINISTRATION
A Devotional and Motivational Guide

Resource Publications
An Imprint of Wipf and Stock Publishers
199 W. 8th Ave., Suite 3
Eugene, OR 97401
www.wipfandstock.com

ISBN 13: 978-1-60899-281-2

Manufactured in the U.S.A.

All Bible quotations are taken from The Living Bible Version and The NIV Study Bible unless marked otherwise.

To all

pastors and laity

in the administration

of the church:

I humbly submit this book so that together we may continue to receive a revelation to do our best in pleasing God through the ministry of leadership and supervision of the church in our times. Use the spanners in this book to fix the ship (church) until it gets to its final destination (eternal salvation).

Amen.

Contents

Preface

THIS BOOK IS WRITTEN for three types of readers. *First*, it is intended to be a lay training manual for pastors and lay persons who are leaders of the church in all denominations in Zimbabwe and beyond our borders. Readers can use it for lay training, leadership seminars, retreats, or personal spiritual reflection. They can also use some parts of the book for devotions during meetings with leaders at all levels within the church structure. *Second*, this is a textbook for use in theological colleges, Bible institutions, and university faculties of theology where church administration, leadership, and pastoral counseling are offered as general introductory courses. *Third*, this book is for the laity that is currently involved in leading the church of God at various levels.

I thank all those who have encouraged and helped me in the process towards publishing this book. It is not possible to mention all of them. However, the following are some without whose assistance this devotional and motivational guide could not have been a reality: Dr. Robert Heaton of the Theological College of Zimbabwe read the manuscript and gave constructive comments, of which I am grateful. I thank Bishop Dr. S. M. Dube of the Evangelical Lutheran Church for his encouraging comments and advice on the practical and administrative aspects of the book. Rev. Dr. Victor Noah, President of the Theological College of Zimbabwe, Bulawayo, went through the book and gave great insights and suggestions of which I am most thankful. I am also very grateful to Rev. Dr. C. J. Machukera, Principal of the United Theological College, Harare, for going through the book and offering some most valuable comments. I also thank S. Mhlanga for the notes on HIV/AIDS, as well as Dr. A. Chivaura on stress management.

My sincere thanks go to Duduzile Mandisodza, Jerison Vuriri, Moses Kalafula, and Qondile Kumalo for proofreading the manuscript and making helpful suggestions. I am humbled by the assistance I got from my wife and friend Tabitha. She read several drafts of the work before publishing. She provided very helpful suggestions and comments, particularly with the chapters Motivation and Pastor's Wife.

I am thankful to all pastors and laity in Bulawayo-Midlands District for helping me soldier on together with them in doing our level best in running the church in challenging times. I am humbled by the guidance and support, as well as the professional and spiritual advice I got from them.

Finally, I thank Bishop Eben K. Nhiwatiwa and his cabinet in The United Methodist Church, Zimbabwe Episcopal Area, first, for inviting me to the cabinet for a six year term (2005–2010) and, second, for assigning me the responsibility of Superintendent for the Bulawayo-Midlands district, which covered Matabeleland North and South, Midlands, and Botswana areas. This has been a challenging task with great opportunities for personal, professional, and spiritual growth that I could never have experienced in a life time.

Clifford Mushishi
Bulawayo, Zimbabwe
June 2010

Prologue

Do all the good you can, by all the means you can, in all the ways you can, in all the places you can, at all the times you can, to all the people you can, as long as ever you can.

—John Wesley, Founder of Methodism

. . . those who preach the Good News should be supported by those who benefit from it.

1 Corinthians 9:14

Leadership is the ability to inspire and turn vision into reality.

—Author Unknown

People don't care how much you know, until they know how much you care.

—John C. Maxwell, Author

The most important ingredient in the formula of success is to know how to get along with people.

—Theodore Roosevelt, American President

". . . we have left our homes and followed you," . . . "Yes," Jesus replied . . . "and I assure you, everyone who has given up house or wife or brothers, or parents or children, for the sake of the Kingdom, will be repaid many times over in this life, as well as receiving eternal life in the world to come."

Luke 18: 29–30

. . . Instead, whoever wants to be great among you must be your servant, and whoever wants to be first must be slave of all. For even the Son of Man did not come to be served, but to serve, and to give his life as a ransom for many.

Mark 10: 44–45

Life is long if you know how to live it.

—Seneca

Commit everything you do to the Lord. Trust him, and he will help you.

Psalm 37:5

There is only one reason why every Christian should be a tither: because it is Biblical.

—R. T. Kendall, Author

I have fought a good fight, I have finished the race, and I have remained faithful. And now the prize awaits me . . .

2 Timothy 4: 7–8

Leaders who aren't getting results aren't truly leading.

—D. Ulrich, J. Zenger, and N. Smallwood, Authors

And God is faithful. He will not let you be tempted beyond your ability, but with the temptation he will also provide the way of escape, that you may be able to endure it.

1 Corinthians 10:13

If your actions inspire others to dream more, learn more, do more and become more, you are a leader.

—John Quincy Adams

It is not only what we do, but also what we do not do, for which we are accountable.

—Moliere

1

Introduction

THE AIM OF THIS book is to share ideas about effective church administration in modern times and contexts. It is a practical guide intended to motivate pastors and other church leaders in the ministry of leadership. To be an effective leader one must anchor all wisdom and faith on Christ. This must be done through prayer, fasting, obedience, and humility.

In this book the church is defined as an organization headed by Christ, the source of our faith. The church is like a body with many parts (1 Cor. 12:12), symbolized here by our different denominations, all doing God's work in various forms. This body must function properly to sustain its purpose of existence. In this text an attempt is made to show how the church must be run efficiently to bring people to Christ, and make him known and be accepted for personal salvation.

The guidelines for effectively running the church, to achieve this goal, are given within the different chapters. Each chapter provides some ideas and guidelines for which the reader can use in supervising the church in any context. The reader has the freedom to add or subtract from the list of suggestions given in the interest of the church. Leadership qualities and styles in the work of the church, for example, are gifts of the Holy Spirit. But it is important for church leaders to always remember to have a special closeness and quiet time with the Holy Spirit to listen attentively and take instructions as required all the time. It may be a temptation for most leaders to keep busy with administrative programs and fail to have special time alone with the Holy Spirit for guidance and direction. If you have no time to read this book, it is enough just to say the prayer at the end of one of the chapters after a difficult meeting or pastoral visit or a great worship service or any situation you consider important. This is important because the pastor must manage God's people with a passion for the ministry through which worship, evangelism, and finance are critical pillars. To lead the church with wisdom, we all must hold on to the cross to provide a leadership that sustains the church to eternity. We must therefore keep our communication lines with God open and direct. All financial administration, pastoral visitation, care and counseling, leadership styles, professional conduct, teachings, and sermons must be anchored on the cross through this open and direct communication.

Several chapters of this book, such as the ones on stress management and motivation, are discussed with a view to sharing tested ideas which can be used in church administration to manage our attitudes, feelings, aspirations, ambitions, and programs in any given circumstances. We must seek God's guidance at every stage of our work. After going through this book, it is possible to teach and train our congregations to witness, reach out, and nurture all souls to a point where the whole world can live like Christ, talk like Christ, sing like Christ, walk like Christ, see like Christ, smile like Christ, hear like Christ, and enjoy eternity like Christ.

Prayer: Loving God, help me to continue your work even in difficult times or the best of times. I trust your presence in all situations. I hold on to your promise that you will always be with me until the end of time. Teach me how to be patient with people and situations all the time, even if I can't change them. Guide me O Lord, I pray. Make me an ambassador for peace and an instrument of healing and reconciliation in all circumstances. Amen.

2

What is Church Administration?

DEFINITION OF CHURCH

BEFORE ANSWERING THE QUESTION: What is church administration? it is important to define the word "church." The word church means assembly. It has its roots in Christ who is the head of the church (Eph 5:23). All administrators of the church today are an extension of this headship. Church administration can therefore be described as a science, an art, and a gift.[1] As a science it involves procedures and techniques that can be learned by study and practice. As an art it calls for relational activity, intuition, and timing. St. Paul said that administration is a spiritual gift (1 Cor 12:28).

Church administration is ministry, not methods.[2] Further, it is people, not paper work. It is human processes, not inhumane policies. It is management, not manipulation. Church administration is helping people and organizations use their resources well.[3] It involves growing people spiritually and professionally, not simply doing things.[4] It operates within a structure where leaders are chosen to administer it (Acts 6:3). Traced from its original meaning "church," in Greek "*ekklesia*," refers to those who are called by a common confession of Jesus Christ as their Lord.

In the Septuagint (earliest translation of the Old Testament), "church" refers to Israel as assembled for religious and cultic purposes (Deut 31, 1 Kgs). As such, Israel is God's chosen race, called for a divine initiative into holy convocation (Gal 6:16). In the New Testament the

1. Powers, ed., *Church Administration Handbook*, 11.
2. Ibid.
3. Ibid.
4. Ibid.

church was created out of the band of disciples associated with the early ministry of Jesus who received the power of the Holy Spirit on the day of Pentecost, empowering them to witness and preach the risen Lord in all places. From this background, the church as we understand it today has taken an outward form of congregations of believers. These believers meet in various places for worship. Today the World Council of Churches defines "church" as an instrument or establishment of God's will within which the mediation of salvation is communicated to humankind.[5]

ADMINISTRATION

Traced from its Latin roots the word "administration" derives from *administrate* which means "to serve." Church administration guides the faith community into realizing its spiritual goals. Administration is therefore a ministry. Functionally, an administrator finds himself leading the way that things must be done in any organization. Or, for example, a leader often finds himself or herself involved in the administration of the church he or she leads. Administration in the church requires several sets or combinations of qualities including but not limited to humility, firmness, an active sense of accountability, responsibility, action oriented, time consciousness, well temperedness, spiritual maturity, giftedness in effective communication, selflessness, reliability, worthy of trust, and God fearing. The *purpose* of administration in the church is *discovering* and *clarifying* goals. The purpose for the existence of the church is providing direction to the church or congregation. Church administration refers to a process of *directing* or *leading* the people of God to realize their goals in serving the Lord through the church that they have chosen to be members.[6] The administration of the church is God-centered (theocentric) and people-oriented[7] (anthrocentric). Other forms of administration, which are not the church, are centered on their organizations and have less or no focus on the spiritual aspect of life. Church administration is a *discipline* of the Holy Spirit.

The purpose of church administration is to make known the love of God to humankind through well-organized spiritual programs. In addition, the phrase "church administration" refers to guiding the church to achieve its goals of witnessing the risen Christ to the world.

5 Douglas, ed., *New International Dictionary*, 227.

6. Lindgren, *Foundations for Purposeful Church Administration*, 14.

7. Ibid.

LEADERSHIP

In general, leadership is the capacity and will to rally men and women to believe in a common purpose and character which inspires confidence, as noted by the British Field Marshal, Bernard Montgomery.[8] It means showing the way—not just the way but the right way. Sometimes it is often said that you can measure a leader by the problems he tackles.[9] He often looks for ones his own size.[10] To administer the church is to lead and give direction and guidance to the church on behalf of God Himself.

Christian leadership means *influencing* people to do what God desires them to do for the good of the church in response to the church's spiritual objectives. To lead is to be ahead of others that are following. Leading means guiding the course of events and programs. To lead is to set a pace of how and what must be done, and why as well as when. So the leader must always be ahead of the people he or she is leading in thought, perception, planning, and organization of the church. To lead is to be in front, breaking new ground, conquering new worlds, and moving away from the status quo.[11] Aim to do better. Great leaders must never be satisfied with current levels of performance.[12] For example, a great preacher must aim to be a better preacher than his homiletics professor. Preachers must constantly strive for higher and greater levels of achievement; move beyond the status quo; and ask the same for those around them.[13]

Church administration must help the congregation realize set objectives. All church administrators and leaders must make a difference. This means communicating and interacting with the congregation but not commanding it. Leading the church means guiding spiritual programs that bring people to Christ. The administrator must therefore not be in doubt as to what needs to be done by the church at every stage of its life. Church leaders are expected to know everything about the church even though they may, in fact, not be able to know everything.

8 Maxwell, *21 Indispensable Qualities of a Leader,* 1.

9. Ibid.

10. Ibid.

11. Maxwell, *4 Pillars of Leadership*, 100.

12. Ibid.

13. Ibid.

They are expected to have all answers even though it is not possible for any human being to have all answers to all peoples' questions. Church leaders must ask God to lead them so they can lead others. Ask God to show the way, the truth, and the life so others can follow this pattern of the faith journey.

POLITY OF THE CHURCH

Polity of the church means government of the church. Church polity refers to the way the church governs itself. This includes, for instance, how the denominations have come into existence or how are they instituted or who elects the leaders; what criteria are used for such an election and how long each elected leader keeps the post before the next leader is elected for the same post; and the description of the appointment system of officers of the church. Polity involves the way the church is governed in terms of financial and human resources. What are the electoral laws and spiritual framework of operation for the denomination upon which decisions are anchored? How is authority perceived by the entire membership of the denomination? This is church polity. The church has laws, a constitution, regulations that govern the parameters of operation, and systems that are followed to achieve certain objectives within a given period of time by certain persons with certain types of qualifications.

Every congregation in the world today has its own tradition. It has its peculiar way of running the spiritual and temporal affairs of its own faith community. The political terrain of each denomination is different from the other. The policies for each denomination are very different from those of other church denominations. In some churches, for example, an individual can become a bishop only after attaining the age of forty-five. In others, one just has to be an ordained elder to take responsibility for such an office. In some churches, baptism is supposed to be done by an ordained priest, while in others an appointed leader can perform that function.

The first and most important thing for any pastor appointed to any church to do is to understand in great detail the policies of the church as defined in the constitution (book of law or regulations) of that church. Just as lawyers must know the constitution of the state in which they practice law or teachers must be familiar with the syllabus to be followed in any teaching program or medical doctors must know the prescription for a patient, so the pastor must know the polity of the church where he is pastor. There is nothing as bad for a pastor than to misquote a passage from the constitution of his church or Bible only to be corrected by a lay person. This is very embarrassing for the clergy. Know the polity of your church and lead the congregation well in order to achieve its objectives. If you are not sure, ask your supervisor to give you guidance.

In addition to knowing the polity or constitution of the church in which you are a pastor, get to understand how the members that you lead interpret and understand the church in which they are members. Ask them what they understand to be the polity of the church. This is critical for you as an administrator because you may be worlds apart. The gap between what you know and what they consider to be vital in the polity of the church may affect the way both of you will run the church. The gap sometimes results in misunderstanding or confusion. So, understanding is a key aspect of effective administration of any congregation.

PLANNING AND ORGANIZING

Our Lord Jesus Christ made a significant plan when he was to have the Passover meal with his disciples (Mark 14:12–26). He sent an advance party to the venue of the meeting—ahead of the rest—with planning instructions. They were to find a man carrying a jar of water and were to follow him. They were to ask him where the Lord was to meet with his disciples. He showed them the place. It is very logical to conclude that the Lord could have made prior plans before the meeting although the Bible does not mention this. This was not the time when the Lord made skillful planning for the work of God. At another stage of his ministry people made plans for his travel. One family provided a donkey for him to ride on when he entered the city of Jerusalem. We should never underestimate the value and importance of planning as part of success in ministry. All successful churches and pastors plan their work well ahead of time to avoid hasty decisions and confusion. Plan what you want to do well ahead of time to avoid last minute pressures for all your church programs. Planning is one certain way of ensuring successful ministry.

To plan is to identify what you want to do for yourself or your organization in order to achieve set goals or objectives. No business or organization can work effectively without planning the way things must go. At the beginning of every year the church must be led into deciding what goals need to be achieved in terms of the mission and ministry of the church.

Virtually all our work, including planned sermons, must lead people to Christ. When people come to church, give them Christ! Other things like entertainment are the responsibility of other clubs not church. So the golden rule in every sound church administration is planning your work. Planning is not just scribbling things on paper. It involves determination, making tough decisions, implementing difficult policies, and doing complicated processes of self evaluation, which most administrators hate.

Planning, therefore, entails identifying what needs to be done. For example, we all know that the work of the church is to bring people to Christ and to take care of their spiritual and physical needs such as good health and social security. We must plan methods for how people must be brought to Christ within a given period. Any church that does not plan for the number of people it will need to bring to Christ is operating just a club or burial society, where people are worried about their bones and flesh only. What happens to their souls in the afterlife may not be a priority in the first instance.

So, planning for any church or congregation is important. Planning involves the scheming of a program, whose goals are guided by a time frame. This is also the way God himself operates in the world that he created. For example, he says to Abraham: by this time next year you will have a child. God here demonstrates that he plans to achieve goals at appointed times. In turn his people develop great confidence in him as their father. An administrator who plans and fulfils his planned objectives earns the confidence of the people that he leads. Be sensitive to planning. Do not just let things happen. Planning is an art that must be learned and be developed. Gifted planners the world over are great achievers of their goals. They live happier and longer lives because they are not stressed by having to cope with piles of unattended files, unplanned visits, budgets, bills, meetings and emergencies.

The critical question for any church denomination that is involved in effective planning should be: what do we hope to achieve by the end of a certain period and how do we achieve that? In any church program planning, the following questions and obligations must guide the administrator: What is the purpose of this organization? How do you order the church to function as a coordinated unit? People who move the organization must be convened for the purpose of implementing plans and programs for the efficient running of the church. The time frame for achieving set goals must be well clarified. What must be specifically achieved in a given period? What resources are available to achieve set goals? Who are the people to be assigned to achieve these goals? How much time must pass before an evaluation is called to check progress? These questions apply for any business or organization if it is to run efficiently. No matter how unique an administrative situation may be, effective planning that involves these questions yields some meaningful results.

IMPLEMENTING

Most church denominations have a hierarchy that stretches from the highest office of the bishop or president to the lowest church leader. Planning strategies run from top to bottom. This is where the conferencing system originates. Policy decisions are made from the top and then flow in a descending way down to the smaller churches. This is called devolution or decentralization. All pastors are part of this structure. They then implement all decisions that are made from top to bottom in the hierarchy of the church. Whenever any part of the structure is weak the whole system will break down.

One of the most effective ways an administrator of the church can be assured of good leadership is to implement church programs without delay. Never sit on a file or a letter when it gets into your office. Take action in the next twenty seconds! The worst administrators in the world today never reply to letters on time. They never return calls that came in their absence. They sit on messages meant for their attention. They postpone meetings at random. They implement programs through pressure from colleagues. They delegate every aspect of their work to other people as if they are so generous, when, in fact, the opposite may be true.

A good administrator must never be reminded of what to implement by his supervisor or by colleagues. If you need to be reminded of your responsibility, it simply means you are not supposed to be in that position because you are not paid to forget but to remember to do things at the right time. Forgetful leaders make life difficult for other people who work with them because deadlines may be missed just because of one person.

COMMUNICATING

Communication in the church is the ministry of sharing the church's story with the public. This helps the church to create an image of itself. We build communities of faith in this special way. Communication is the relaying of information and material from one point of the organization to another through what we do, say, and show. It is not just what one says that matters, but how it is said and who says it. Acceptability is critical in communication. Certain objectives can be rejected sometimes because they have been presented by inappropriate people. Jesus, the most remarkable communicator the world has ever known, showed a striking ability to choose his words to suit particular individuals, audiences, and occasions. Consider what he says to the Samaritan woman or to Nicodemus or to the blind man or to the woman with a blood issue for twelve years.

The most critical function of an administrator is effective communication between and among members of the organization. In the church, communication is vital for the success of the work of the church. Telephones, faxes, newsletters, the internet, text messages, pulpit announcements, flyers, brochures, television, personal visits, celebrations, church directory, letters, logo, database, invitational Sundays, voicemail, clothing with slogans or logo, bumper stickers, newspaper adverts and releases, yellow pages, special events, radio broadcast, pamphlets, website, table displays, and signs form part of the modern ways of communication.

EVALUATING

To evaluate is to take stock of whether the set objectives of an organization such as the church have been achieved. This is done in order to inform the church whether it is still on course or not. The aim of evaluation is to establish whether the methods used to achieve some set goals were appropriate. If they were, more could still be done using the same methods. If they were not, some method changes may need to be effected. For example, if the goal of the congregation was to bring five people to Christ and only one person was saved, then an examination of the method used has to be carried out to find out why this objective was not achievable in terms of expected numbers. If one of the methods was to organize a crusade, for instance, was it well attended or well timed in terms of the other calendar events of the church or the government? Were the preachers appropriate? How can it best be done in the future to achieve maximum results?

Any pastor who plans his work properly must have time to evaluate what he has planned. At the highest level of the church or denomination this evaluation is critical. Some denominations work, or program their work, in terms of quadrennial or five year development plans and visions. What have we achieved in the just ending quadrennium? is an appropriate question to ask for such churches that use this pattern.

What difference am I making? is a question every pastor must ask all the time when serving a congregation. This motivates the pastor to administer the congregation with an anticipation of success in leadership and spiritual development of the denomination, infrastructural development, and meaningful benchmarks. When a pastor has been elevated to a higher post of superintendent or bishop or president it is unavoidable that the church will expect meaningful change in the life of that denomination or district. Other leaders are good at maintaining what others have initiated. It is OK but not good enough. Develop and leave a mark from where your colleagues left. In terms of leadership, develop initiatives for new and further training in the work of ministry and allocate funds for them to realize this initiative.

In terms of developing facilities for social services, missionaries taught us that the church must buy property, such as farms, and build houses, hostels, schools, and hospitals. This way you can develop the lives of ordinary people. You touch their lives in an effective and lasting way. I am not quite sure how many denominations have bought new properties for the church after the missionary era. Most appear to be maintaining what the missionaries labored to put up, while others have failed to maintain even that.

All of us in the church must seek to create something new for the churches that we serve, not for churches to create new things for us. If churches overseas must help us, we must be already working hard to sustain the church in our community.

The following[14] can make you a successful person in your church administration:

1. Clarify your objectives.
2. Establish priorities that match your objectives.
3. Break the main tasks into little pieces and start on them immediately.
4. Clean up your paperwork daily.
5. Learn to say no to important requests that do not fit your objectives.

Prayer: Dear Lord, help me to lead and administer the church in your way, not mine. Grant me the sense and opportunity to know the difference. Help me to accept challenges and problems as learning experiences. Amen.

14 Miller, *Leadership is the Key*, 70.

3

Administration of the Local Church

WHAT IS A LOCAL CHURCH?

THE PHRASE "LOCAL CHURCH" refers to a given geographical boundary within which a part of the faith community assembles for worship. In most denominations a local church is the smallest organized unit for purposes of worship. Some denominations define local church as "parish" while others simply refer to it as "congregation". So, local church in this chapter is understood to mean local parish or congregation within a given locality or community. The local church then is made up of various family households. The local church is a community of believers and a redemptive fellowship where divinely called persons are appointed to minister the word in all forms approved.[1] The local church has three major functions: (a) to engage in worship, (b) to edify the believers, and (c) to redeem the world.[2] The local church is a strategic base from which Christians can move out to the structures of the society by defending God's creation and nurturing the community.[3] There is no fixed rule as to how families or members can make up a local church, although for most churches twenty full members can constitute a local church.

HOW DO YOU START A NEW LOCAL CHURCH?

The following guidelines are found to be convenient for the starting of a local church in most mainline denominations such as the United Methodist Church. Other denominations have other forms and methods

1. Book of Discipline, *United Methodist Church*, 127.
2. Ibid.
3. Ibid., 27–28.

that apply in their polity governing the starting of a new congregation. The following would apply in the case of a United Methodist setting:

a) The members themselves must be in agreement that they can start a local church.
b) The mother church or congregation must have approved the plan to start a local church.
c) The number of full members must not be less than twenty. Practical experience has shown that twenty full members who financially support the budget without question can manage a local church without strain.
d) There must be a leadership in place to lead the faith community.
e) The community of faith must have been in existence for at least a year.
f) Study the geography and politics of your local church.
g) The financial state of the faith community must be sound.
h) The probationary members must be committed too, just like the full members in terms of faith and financial strength.

HOW DO YOU KNOW YOUR LEADERS?

The first thing a pastor must do when appointed to a local congregation is to get to know the leaders. If it is a new congregation, study how it came about and who were the particular leaders at the time of inception. This is important to know because the strength of a congregation is measured by the strength of its leadership. Study the areas of strength and praise the leaders. Study the mistakes made at the initial setting of the local church and leadership, if any. Learn from these errors without condemning anyone for them. If you have to help the congregation elect leaders, guide the church to make informed choices and let them decide the period within which the elected leaders must serve before the next ballot.

If you found the congregation already in existence upon your appointment, get to know the leaders as fast as possible. You can interview them on a one on one basis or invite them to an informal dinner or get-together, to have a clear understanding of what they feel must be done to make this particular congregation the best place for anyone to be, in terms of spiritual comfort and social service provision. After interviewing each of the leaders, you will obviously be able to make a decision as to how certain problems, if any, can be solved. The interviews will also give you an idea from which to start ministering to the real needs of the congregation. If the leaders are well trained laypersons, they must be in a position to advise the pastor in the best way.

UNPROFESSIONAL PRACTICE WHEN APPOINTED TO A NEW CONGREGATION

1. Avoid criticizing your predecessor in public. Learn from what has been done. Take time to understand the way your predecessor was operating. If he or she made mistakes, apologize on his or her behalf for the good of the church. Do not waste time by discussing the mistakes of the other pastor who came before you. Instead, build on each other's work and gain confidence from both the strengths and the areas that needed to be improved by your predecessor. Listen and then make your own conclusions. Do not get excited about the previous pastor's mistakes; instead, pray about them and seek God's guidance in avoiding a repeat of them. If the congregation was hurt by some decisions that have taken place in error, your immediate task as a pastor is to heal the wounds.

2. Do not make the church feel embarrassed for not adequately furnishing the parsonage. Instead, teach them gradually to develop from where they are to greater heights. It is not wise to blame the congregation for failing to own a house or any other property. Instead, teach them and work hard with them so they may know what house or property purchase that you feel a congregation needs to have.

3. When you leave that local church never take what belongs to the church. Refer to the inventory that they must have asked you to sign before you entered the parsonage. Small items such as cell phones, curtains, blankets, pillows, and flowerpots are very tempting to take with you when you leave, so watch out for this bad practice.

4. Do not change leadership abruptly. Take time to learn about the congregation: its strengths, weaknesses, habits, tendencies, traditions, culture, expectations, limitations, and immediate challenges. If there is pressure on you to mount such a change in leadership, pray about it, then manage the pressure and put it before your entire leadership or congregation for them to make a decision on this important matter. Even if you have your own position, give them a chance to contribute to the overall decision.

5. If the congregation owes the previous pastor or the mother church any money or goods and services, make it a priority to get this settled before you benefit from their support. This will lead the church to appreciate the importance of meeting such obligations on time.

6. Do not search for the weaknesses of those people in the leadership, but instead search for what they can do best and build on them with mature confidence.

STUDY THE FLOCK AND ITS NEEDS

When appointed to a new local church, take time to study the flock or the membership. This will help you to shepherd them in an effective way. The following practices may help to create a good rapport with the membership:

1. Earn trust and confidence from the congregation by involving them in all activities of which they are part.

2. Command respect by the way you conduct yourself in speech, dress, consistency, the way you talk to them about other people, caring attitude, and sense of humor.

3. Check on what the congregation hates most and what the people like most and find out the reasons for both positions.

4. Take time to find out where most of the members spend their free time. Attempt to visit them at such places. This will help you understand the way the congregation behaves in public and in private.

5. Suggest informal gatherings such as potlucks or couples' or single parents' fellowships with them to create closer relations with them and check their views on this move.

6. Take an inventory of who is in business and what type of business (formal or informal), and who is in college and for what courses. Get to know what percentage of the membership is involved in what activities. This is important because what they do every day affects the way they behave and react to situations on events that take place in the church at any given time.

7. Find out which members find it hard to support the church and why. Talk to them separately and try to understand what they say. Appreciate their pattern of life and work with them while considering both their way of looking at life and living the gospel of Jesus Christ in their way.

8. Study the life patterns of those who give most in the church. Take time to talk to them and find out why they place giving to God as the first priority in their life. What have they seen of Godthat has touched their life to the extent that they always want to honor God through their wealth?

9. Make a list of those who come to church but never want to fellowship or participate in any of the programs, including giving. Find out why they do not feel they should participate in worship in this manner.

10. Visit every member in their home within the first six months of your appointment of this local church. This is the most significant way of knowing your flock.

MEMBERSHIP CARE METHODS

There are several methods that can be employed to care for church membership. The following is a general list of such methods:

1. Know each of the members by name.

2. Know all the members by location. This means that you have to know where they stay by visiting them frequently.

3. As the pastor of the congregation, personally draw up the membership list. The membership list must include: name of person, date of birth, place of birth, date of baptism, officiating pastor at the baptism—or date of confirmation, or date of reception into the church, or date of withdrawal and reason—and any other information that will help the pastor to fully know his members.[4]

4. Pray for the members personally by name.

5. Identify each member by need in his family and personal life.

6. Give the congregation sermons that uplift everyone all the time.

7. Take great interest in what each member does in life and remember it.

8. Take time to visit and pray with each member at his work place.

9. Meet groups that have the same interests once in a while for informal discussions.

10. Telephone or text a message of hope to each of the members and even quote a scripture verse to uplift them in their spiritual life, especially those who come to church as couples.

11. Identify big givers, average ones, and non-participating ones and pray for each one of them by name.

4. Ibid.

12. Identify in each member some significant talent such as preaching, giving, exhorting, prophesying, teaching, providing social services, or caregiving. Approach them and encourage them to not hide their talents.

13. Encourage each member to inform you if they are visiting friends or family members away from the local church for an extended period. Write and give them a letter confirming their visit away from the rest to give to the next pastor in the locality where they will be visiting. This is pastoral care by extension where a member in one congregation is taken care of by the next pastor while he is on a visit. For more extended periods, the member can be asked to take an affiliate or associate membership status. This means the member has all the membership rights while he is away from his usual congregation.

14. Encourage each member to write a will while they are still alive.

15. Encourage each member to provide an endowment from their estate for the church. It may be cash for a scholarship in their memory, or immovable property.

16. When any member is removed from the roll by death make sure a memorial service is conducted for him by the church.

17. Annually organize a memorial service for all those members in your congregation who had died. Invite family members to celebrate their late relative's life with the church.

18. Keep all church records on electronic media or in a membership record book. When you leave the congregation advise the incoming pastor, in writing, where these records will be stored.

19. When you leave the congregation leave notes on the table for the next pastor. Preferably leave the membership record book on the pastor's desk. Include brief notes on the table where they should be visible for your colleague. The notes must be pointers to relevant information pertaining to the office. They must tell the next pastor where to find relevant information, such as: the list of current or outgoing leaders; holy communion material; state of the local church statement; membership trends; projects achieved in the last two years; ongoing projects and the officers of the church who are spearheading them; what you failed to achieve and the reasons why you think you could not succeed in this area; major problems you faced in terms of membership drive; and your vision for the next five years. This gives the next pastor a rough

idea of the status and goals of the congregation before he talks to any of the officers listed on the leadership list. He will start from a fairly good administrative terrain. The notes must wish the next pastor well in his tenure of office.

20. Take time to fast for your members, especially those in difficult times. But never tell them you are in a fasting program for them unless you want them to join you in this spiritual program.

MANAGEMENT OF WORSHIP AND PULPIT SUPPLY

One of the most important roles of the pastor in supervising the spiritual program of the local church is to lead the congregation in worship. The pastor should supply the pulpit with sermons that uplift, encourage, rebuke in love, and comfort the believers. This happens through prayer, fasting, and preaching. One way of doing this is to make sure the sermons are well prepared at least thirty days before the day of the actual preaching. This gives you enough time for research, meditation, and reflection. For every sermon (long or short) the following guidelines must apply for a good sermon:

A. Standard Sermon Guidelines

The sermon must have three parts: The Introduction, Central Message and Conclusion.

1. Introduction:

    1.1. Is the preacher dressed appropriately?
    Yes
    No

    1.2. Was the sermon introduced?
    Yes
    No

    1.3. Was there any theme announced?
    Yes
    No

    1.4. Was the theme clear?
    Yes
    No

    1.5. Was the theme short?
    Yes
    No

1.6. Was the bible reading clear?
   Yes
   No
1.7. Has the text been explained?
   Yes
   No
1.8. Has any instrument been used to attract the attention of the audience?
   Yes
   No

2. Central message:

2.1. Is the theme sustained in the central message?
   Yes
   No
2.2. Are the points orderly?
   Yes
   No
2.3. Is there an illustration in the sermon?
   Yes
   No
2.4. Did the illustration help clarify the message?
   Yes
   No
2.5. Is the message being understood?
   Yes
   No
2.6. Are you moving with the audience?
   Yes
   No
2.7. What signs have you seen to show that the audience is attentive?
   a.
   b.
2.8. What signs have you seen to show that you have lost your audience?
   a.
   b.

3. Conclusion:

   3.1. Has the conclusion been announced?
   Yes
   No

   3.2. Is the conclusion a safe landing?
   Yes
   No

   3.3. Was the illustration linked to the message?
   Yes
   No

   3.4. Was the message clear?
   Yes
   No

   3.5. Were the Bible reading and the hymns relating to the message?
   Yes
   No

   3.6. Could anyone summarize the sermon in one word or phrase?
   Yes
   No

   3.7. Did you give any instruction to the audience at the end of the sermon?
   Yes
   No

   3.8. Were you in control of the audience throughout the sermon?
   Yes
   No

B. Types of sermons

There are several types of sermons that one can use to deliver God's message. Below are some of them. The list is not exhaustive. [NL 1–5]

1. ***Social sermon***: This type of sermon focuses on social problems and issues such as corruption, poverty, wealth, morals, crime, and justice among others. Material relating to the prophet Amos and others are most suitable for such sermons. Any part of scripture, however, can be used for a social sermon.
2. ***Evangelical sermon***: This type of sermon focuses on evangelizing people and communities to surrender their lives to Christ. Such types of biblical texts such as the call of Isaiah chapter 6 or Jeremiah chapter 1 or any passage in the New Testament could be used to preach an evangelistic sermon.
3. ***Teaching sermon***: Most of the sermons preached by our Lord Jesus Christ were teaching sermons. A teaching sermon provides spiritual instruction. It aims to achieve doing good, living in harmony with God and fellow human beings, and to stay in love with God as John Wesley suggested.
4. ***Prophetic sermon***: This type of sermon focuses on the preacher pronouncing what God is saying to people through him or her. Early time prophets would say: "Thus says the Lord . . ." This is not different from an ethical or social sermon in that it addresses social issues in society as the prophet gets to understand them in God's eyes.
5. ***Philosophical sermon***: This type of sermon focuses on rationality or on an idea that causes people and communities to see, hear, think, feel, and realize God within their reasoning capacities. An abstract idea can be used to make people understand what God is doing among us. A sermon can be formed from riddles.

C. Methods of preaching

1. Bible stories
2. Textual interpretation
3. Slides
4. Day-to-day stories

5. Interactive preaching
6. Lecture
7. Personal testimony
8. Historical events
9. Scientific developments
10. Mass media: print or electronic
11. Picture work
12. One-to-one witnessing
13. Group counseling
14. Group discussions

D. Embarrassing mistakes to avoid while preaching

1. Forgetting a bible passage
2. Lack of order
3. Mismatch of text, hymn, illustration, and message
4. Inappropriate sense of humor
5. Anger
6. Overexcitement
7. Grudging
8. Crying
9. Repetition
10. Entertainment
11. Lack of gender sensitivity
12. Lack of respect for audience
13. Excessive jokes
14. Intimidation

E. Sermon checklist before and after preaching

1. The sermon must also preach to you as a preacher. As you prepare it, you must receive a new revelation or truth about the word of God.
2. There must be a match between the bible reading, the message, the choir songs, the hymnals, and the theme of the sermon.
3. The sermon must have a one word (or phrase or sentence) theme or topic or title. Long themes are hard to remember. Be short and to the point.
4. The sermon must have an illustration such as a story, drama, biography, or character which helps your message to become more vivid or clearer to your audience. Not more than two or three illustrations are recommended to avoid loss of meaning for your message.
5. The sermon must help someone in the congregation, for example, causing one to convert or uplift them spiritually or heal a wounded soul or body.
6. The sermon must be simple for all age groups to understand. Mind your language. Are you communicating or just talking to yourself?
7. The sermon must give the audience something to take home. They must summarize your message in one word or phrase after the worship service.
8. The sermon must give glory and credit to God.
9. Avoid pride. You are just an instrument to witness the glory of God.
10. Avoid entertaining stories that have little or no bearing on the message. Apply the stories to your message. The stories must not override or overshadow the message.
11. Whisper a thank you to the Lord after your sermon, never mind which way it went!

PROFESSIONAL CONDUCT FOR PASTORS STARTING OR LEAVING A CONGREGATION[5]

The administration of professional conduct for pastors who start, or leave a congregation for another appointment for one reason or another, must be handled with care. This is because all congregations share information

5. For more details on the commandments for pastors leaving pastorates, see Farris, "*Ten Commandments for Pastors Leaving a Congregation.*"

informally (and formally) about the pastor they are either getting or the one who has transferred from their station. Some people call this gossip. Other people call it the "latest" (news). The way you conduct yourself as a new pastor in the first six months will be under examination by your members in order to match or compare you with your colleague. The members do this to confirm what they have heard about you. So it is very important for you to keep a good record about your ministry and administration of people and your interpersonal skills. When you leave a congregation be proud to do so and be ready to return if required to do so. The following issues that affect pastoral relations, such as personal conflicts or friendship with members, must be handled with care. They must not be overdone. Keep a professional distance. When you start or leave a congregation, watch out for the following concerns:

1. Thou shalt know when it is time to go: "For everything there is a season, and a time for every purpose under heaven" (Ecc 3:1).

There is no pastor who is destined to stay at one congregation forever. Long pastorates can be very valuable in establishing congregational stability, but they can also create two challenges: a) comfortable lethargy and b) inability to accept any new style of pastoral leadership by the congregation. So changes in pastorates are critical for servant leadership. Once you have arrived the next thing to prepare for is to leave. Prepare for retirement all the time you are in a congregation. Be actively aware of this feature. It is a good thing to leave before being asked to move by the administration or the congregation. It is very easy to sense if people feel they still need you around.

2. Thou shalt explain thyself: "About this we have much to say which is hard to explain" (Heb 5:11a).

Pastors have a great task of explaining things to congregations if any move is being made in or against their favor. Congregations are entitled to such explanations because they are stakeholders in terms of congregational support. They are part of the church in every respect. The clergy can never run the church by itself. Neither can the laity.

3. Thou shalt not take with you what does not belong to you: "You shall not steal" (Exod 20:15).

One of the worst things a pastor can do to a congregation is to cheat it. Get paid for services you never provided! Get travel allowances for a journey you never made! Inflate figures for a trip you never accomplished! Make a claim for a meal you never took! Claim hotel expenses for free accommodation that was negotiated! Again, it is a matter of conscience. This is one of the ways in which pastors become beggars forever. Just the sin of dishonesty, it will cost the pastor an entire eternity.

When you leave a congregation, take with you only that which belongs to you according to the trustees of the congregation. Revisit the list before you depart and clarify the separation between the property of the church and your own. Leave everything in good condition just the way you would love to see the same property in the next congregation. Clean the house as you would expect in your next station. Leave the car serviced. Leave the fridge and the stove in good working order. Do not take any property of the church as compensation for an outstanding payment that was due to you. If there is such outstanding money owed to you by the congregation, use the proper administrative channels to claim it in a more professional way, much later after you have left the congregation. Aim to leave amicably through a friendly farewell that must be tension free. This will create room for more blessings on your part.

4. Thou shalt affirm thy congregation's ministry: "We give thanks to God always for you all, constantly mentioning you in our prayers, remembering before our God and Father your work of faith and labour of love and steadfastness of hope" (1 Thess 1:2–3).

When you leave a congregation, affirm those areas of ministry that have made the lifeline of the congregation. Affirm the warm worship services, the bereavement counseling conducted, healing services that brought results, the development of an intercessory prayer ministry that you have started together, the newsletter you have successfully launched, the fellowship groups you have worked hard on, and the many other activities that must be affirmed. Celebrate on your successes rather than your failures. Your successes will help you build your self-esteem. These will also motivate you to work even harder.

5. Thou shalt try to mend fences: "God through Christ reconciled us to himself, and gave us the ministry of reconciliation" (2 Cor 5:18)

There is no pastor in the world that has been successful in pleasing every church member in any given congregation. All of us try, sometimes in vain. The more you stay in a congregation the more enemies and friends you create. It is a principle of life. The idea is to maintain a balance between what you feel God is saying and your conscience in relation to the people you work with. Some can hate you for personality differences, others do not like you for comments you made when there was a crisis. You may have made statements that hurt their feelings during a funeral of their friend or relative unknowingly, or knowingly, and this can create a source of dislike for the pastor. Never carry these grudges with you to the next congregation as they will hound you forever. Be reconciled to yourself and to God, and call those you feel that hate you on to the altar of God's grace for reconciliation with Christ.

6. Thou shalt help thy successor have a good beginning: "Write the vision, make it plain upon tablets, so he may run who reads it." (Hab 2:2).

The most important way to introduce your successor to the new pastorate is to leave a map and a brief history of that congregation on the desk. All other things will follow in their realm as time unfolds. You can also leave contact phone numbers for the key leaders of the church and the community. This will help the new pastor to settle into his initial stages on the major aspects of the congregation. The following list may be helpful for your fellow pastor to see where to start from when you leave the congregation:

a) a copy of the congregation's history;
b) an account of major projects: current and recently completed ones;
c) a copy of current budget;
d) an evaluation of congregation's strengths and weaknesses (and your own weaknesses such as time keeping, failure to attend Sunday school or prepare lessons for those wanting to become members of the church, impatience, lack of pastoral care, and visitation);
e) a list of every family that lost a member in the congregation in the preceding year;
f) a list of preachers and calendar;
g) a membership record;

h) a list of community boards and functions for which you were a member;
i) a description of problems in the community affecting your membership;
j) the names of the nearest doctor or health service, shops, or bus stop.

7. Thou shalt attend to thy family: "Is there anyone among you who, if your child asks for bread, will give a stone? Or if the child asks for a fish, will give a snake"? (Matt 7:9–10).

One of the most painful experiences for pastors is when a transfer is to be effected, especially when they are not ready for it. This means you have to move the children from one school to another. The family has to change a doctor or medical facilities to suit the new environment. The family will have to create new friends. It is a time that needs a lot of prayer and adjustment. The trick is to accept the change with an understanding of the system of your denomination. Other denominations use a system whereby congregations invite pastors to their congregation. If the congregation is no longer interested, they will ask for a change. Slow to acceptance will cause a lot of stress on you. You must counsel your family to accept the change before the change affects their attitude towards the church for the rest of life. Take time to explain how the system works. Do not take it for granted that they understand it. Accept bitter questions and provide answers that are helpful in terms of giving hope. Accept outbursts from your children and your spouse especially if they are not ready for the change. Pray about it in your own private time with the Lord. Concentrate on the brighter side of things than on the negative. The negative will affect your health if not attended to. If you feel the new appointment is not appropriate, approach the administration and explain the difficulty you are facing in accommodating family sentiments. Sharing is part of healing the feelings of hurt and intolerance, as well as discomfort. An alternative appointment may be generated only out of such sharing of exactly how you feel about the change in appointment. There is no way you can be happy as a pastor when the rest of your family is unhappy.

8. Thou shalt stay away once thou hast left: "But Lot's wife, behind him, looked back, and she became a pillar of salt" (Gen 19:26).

When you have left a congregation, never pastor it in absentia. Give meaningful space to the new pastor. Do not pass comments about his work. Do not visit his members unless he invites you. Stay away for better or for worse. Your uninvited presence in your previous congregation creates problems for the new pastor. If you wish to help, call the new pastor and communicate on a professional level showing him areas that you feel may be helpful for him to attend to. If you hear something negative about your colleague, share in sincerity to save his image and that of the church. Do not come back to conduct healing services or bury members or memorial services without being invited by your colleague.

9. Thou shalt not talk negatively about thy colleague.

All bad pastors talk evil about their colleagues. They backbite. They have nothing to contribute to the positive aspects of the work done by other people. There is no pastor in the world today, neither is there any that ever lived, who is or was perfect in his work at any one point in time. Neither is there a perfect church or administration or system anywhere in the world today. We all work with what is available and strive to improve on what others have built. This is the principle everywhere in the world of administration. When you criticize other people for their mistakes after they have already left the congregation, be aware that others may be discussing even worse mistakes than yours. Why not discuss and build on the strengths of your colleague and learn from his errors. On the latter you can apologize on behalf of the pastoral office if you feel this is a reasonable thing to do. Correct professional errors made before with understanding, love, and passion. Do not be in a hurry to make changes in your leadership. Reserve comments because you may be quoted out of context. Remain focused. Be truthful and respectful always.

10. Thou shalt respect all those in authority and thy colleagues.

Given various pastoral appointive systems in different denominations, every pastor must make an effort to accept all pastoral assignments and appointments as coming from God. Some such appointments may not be comfortable as they may not suit family requirements or expectations. In addition, these appointments which may not be comfortable for certain pastors are potential sources of bitterness and discomfort. But the philosophy of "here I am Lord, send me" must be applicable in all appointive circumstances. Respect all those in charge of these decisions just the way you would expect other people to respect the same decisions when they come from you.

METHODS OF EQUIPPING LEADERS FOR MAXIMUM EFFECTIVENESS

1. Listen empathetically:

Social scientists say that eighty percent of what we communicate is non-verbal. The pastor must use his ears, eyes, and heart to be empathetic in listening to what the congregation is saying. Never take the people for granted. Seek to understand what they say and feel in order to help them achieve planned goals for the work of God.

2. Care personally:

Take time to care about each leader personally. Do not just be interested in the leaders getting things done for you, like a coach just wants a team to win without caring if one player gets hurt. Respond to the particular needs of each team player including pain; joy; anger; and feelings of remorse; and respond to emotions as they occur. This is the only way to gain the confidence, as team players, in your leaders. If they know you care about them, you can send them to do any task on your behalf and they will do it gladly and most effectively. The phrase "most effectively" means the task is carried out on time and properly.

3. Celebrate victories:

Very good coaches throughout the world know how to party. They take their teams out for partying after winning major victories. In ministry celebrate all progress by identifying each individual who has played a role in the success of the tasks set. It motivates leaders to do even better next time. Their morale is kept high by recognition of a victory by the team leader. Affirm personal achievement by recognizing personal victory. Such recognition could be in the form of a celebration of birthdays, anniversaries, and many others special occasions in the life of a person.

4. Strategize plans:

Strategic planning requires four major steps to equip leaders for effective ministry:

a) Focus priorities: Have a sense of what needs to be done first, and why (purpose, vision, mission, and core values).

b) Eliminate roadblocks: As much as possible, watch out for stumbling blocks in your planning.

c) Maximize resources: Use whatever human and financial resources that are available. Know your critical success factors (things that you need in order to succeed).

d) Determine the next step: As much as possible, all plans must have deadlines not dead ends. Be sensitive to such deadlines. Setting time frames for all activities helps any church to work effectively.

The pastor must be a professional person who can read the signs of the times and act accordingly. The work of the church needs a strategic planner. Understand the morale of the leaders and motivate them through the use of incentives that are meaningful. It is a strategy to get things aboveboard.

5. Challenge specifically:

In the work of the church, greater performance is achieved through setting challenging goals of ministry. But this can only be done through: a) clarifying the vision and goals; b) determining the next steps and assignments; and c) setting the next meeting. The meeting must be followed up with a review of what the role of each person is. Review progress; encourage positive achievement; celebrate victories; set new frontiers for success; clarify next steps; agree on plans and time limits; and determine how success will be measured. Pray with your leaders.

SPECIFIC KEYS FOR DEVELOPING LEADERS IN YOUR CONGREGATION

a) Assessment: Determine gifting, abilities, interests, passion, personality, commitment, energy, and time availability.
b) Assignment: Give specific task assignments that are challenging, yet attainable, as Christ did. Take record of what has been assigned.
c) Accountability: Schedule regular reviews of work, in detail, with specific leaders. Be sensitive to detail.
d) Applause: Acknowledge unique contribution with details of such achievement. Avoid generalization.

e) Advancement: Create opportunity for continual professional growth. Encourage your leaders to attend leadership courses and seminars.
f) Assistance: Provide vision, adequate resources, and consistent support for your leaders. Never assume they are doing fine. Probe them to say if they are facing complications.
g) Evaluation: Provide adequate time for evaluating each of your leaders. Give an opportunity for their self-evaluation of the work they are doing in the church. This is not an opportunity for criticizing anyone but a time to say: Did we do certain things correctly and how can we do them even better next time or where did we go wrong and why or how can we improve on the system next time?

LEADERSHIP TRAINING FOR HOUSE (SECTION) PRAYER MEETINGS

One of the most effective ways to strengthen the church anywhere in the world today is fellowship. Through fellowship, Christian families living in one locality draw closer to each other and to God. They will know each other better and learn God's ways in a more effective manner. The pastor is part of the smallest faith community, called "section" in some churches. These are house prayer meetings. The number of members constituting a section may be twelve or more, even less depending on the situation on the ground. It may not be the numbers that matter but what the members do when they meet for prayer meetings. The pastor must be a member of such a small family of faith, while he takes care of the wider church family. In terms of its administration, there must be some leaders chosen by the members themselves to lead the section. These leaders must be trained. The leaders must be full members of the church. Such leaders may include a section leader, a secretary, treasurer, or a committee member. This is a supportive structure for Christian ministry. Their functions may vary depending on what that section of the church wants done in their area to uplift their spiritual life.

Role of the section (house) prayer meeting leader

1. Organize house meetings by preparing a list of the membership names, addresses, and contact phone and e-mail numbers of all the members in that particular section of the local church.

2. Prepare a schedule for house prayer meetings. The schedule must contain the date, venue, preacher or teacher or speaker, and the topic for that particular day. It is the section leader who hands a copy of the schedule to the pastor.
3. Monitor the schedule with meaningful commitment and dedication. This means finding time to examine each member's attendance to prayer meetings, the level of tithes given to the church, and the time keeping for prayer meetings. Make sure that other members of the section are committed to the schedule as well.
4. Organize a section visit or visits within the year to the pastor's house for fellowship. The fellowship socially and spiritually uplifts the pastor in his work. He will have an opportunity to know each of the church members well by interacting with them at section level on a one-on-one basis as opposed to meeting everyone at church on Sunday.
5. Identify and inform the pastor about new persons in the locality who have just arrived. These could be visitors to families within the section or new arrivals in the community.
6. The section leader may organize his section to visit the new persons, just to greet them and inform them that they are welcome in the community and that if they have anything they feel needs the section's attention, they would be welcome to communicate it.
7. Attend to the spiritual concerns of each of the members of the section and inform the pastor about such concerns in a timely manner. These may include loss, misfortune, hospitalization, illness, adoption of a child, and many other concerns.
8. Keep the pastor advised of developments in the section at given intervals in order for him to be effective in his pastoral work.
9. Develop leadership talent in the members of the section by asking them to do certain tasks as Bible reading, leading in worship, teaching new songs, conducting Bible study, teaching a lesson or organizing a trip or fund raising dinner.
10. Encourage all members of the section to attend Christian education seminars, crusades, spiritual and renewal revivals at home or church or away-from-home spiritual fellowship gatherings.

11. Encourage members to donate generously to the church and to give a tithe as the law of the Bible and as a spiritual discipline. The section needs to check the tithe record of each member from time to time and advise the members of the importance of supporting the church in this special way.

12. Encourage the members to fund a project in the church or community. This may be sponsoring a student or feeding street children or finding clothing for an elderly person in the church or community. It could be painting the church or cutting grass on the church yard or paying for the pastor's phone or electricity bill or sending his car for a service once a year. It could be paying for his children's fees or even sending his clothes for dry cleaning twice or thrice a year depending on what each member feels. Open up the communication regarding these opportunities for the section members to express the way they want to participate in the life of the church.

13. Make sure each prayer meeting includes one of the following: worship, Bible study, testimony that uplifts the life of other Christians, learning new songs from your church hymn book, teaching on responsibilities of each member of the church, sermon, pastor in the section, visit to the sick or elderly or orphanage, all day or night prayer, bring and share, guest preacher or speaker, fund raising, or any other activity as the Holy Spirit leads. The section leader must give each member of the section an opportunity to say what he feels the section program must include in its schedule.

14. Encourage members of the section to be admitted into full membership of the church or men, women, youth organizations. Encourage them to join the choir or any society where the section leader feels they can benefit spiritually.

15. Organize the youth or junior church members of the section to lead in worship or Bible study once in a given period.

16. Recognize the birthdays and wedding anniversaries of members of the section. Also, give recognition to past members of the section in the form of a memorial service is spiritually uplifting to the members.

17. Support all local church and connectional obligations of the denomination as required or as the Holy Spirit informs you.

18. Ensure that the secretary keeps all the records of membership, attendance, correspondence, and updated communication from the pastor's office.
19. Advise the treasurer to provide a financial report of the money contributed by the section members and how it is being used for the spiritual work of the section. This must be done from time to time, as shown in the program. Monthly or quarterly reviews are recommended in most churches.
20. Advise the pastor of those members of the section who may be struggling with drugs or alcohol; or those who may be going through divorce or separation or retrenchment so that the pastor may visit and counsel.
21. Keep each member of the section as close to others as possible—happy, committed, and God fearing through each member's involvement in the program-making process.

HOW DO YOU CHAIR A CHURCH MEETING?

All church meetings are the same whether chaired by the bishop or superintendent or pastor or lay leader or a church steward. This is because they are all about God's business. The level may differ but they must:

a) Start with a prayer.
b) Read minutes of a previous similar meeting (if there was one).
c) Approve of the minutes.
d) Find if there are any matters arising from the minutes, including corrections.
e) Adopt a motion to move the minutes as a correct record of previous proceedings.
f) Adopt an agenda for the new business of the day or meeting.
g) Adopt the agenda with or without amendments.
h) Walk through items on the agenda.
i) Conclude each item discussed with an action.
j) Identify dates for the action plan.
k) Identify date for the next meeting.
l) Appreciate the people for attending the meeting.
m) Close with a prayer.

It is important to note that as a leader one *must not*:

a) Come to the meeting without a paper and pen; a bible, and a hymn book.
b) Over-allocate time to the same person to contribute in the discussions.
c) Forget important dates.
d) Forget important decision of the last meeting.
e) Forget important tasks given in the last meeting.
f) Forget to read the minutes of the previous meeting before the current one.
g) Use emotional language, show anger, or shout at people when chairing.

Prayer: Heavenly Father, advise me to look after your people with a caring attitude. Help me to love them as they are, not the way I wish to see them. Give me the patience to be a good shepherd forever. Amen.

4

Teaching People How to Accept Christ

WHAT IS ACCEPTING CHRIST?

Accepting Jesus Christ as Lord and personal Saviour takes a lot of thought. It is a bold decision one has to make. It is not like deciding to go to the shops to buy bread or soap or milk and then come back home. It demands your conscience, feelings, mindset, and careful examination of what God has done for you in an entire life. It involves losing friends, business, and personal characteristics that you were at peace with but were not in God's favor. Accepting Christ is like getting thirsty. You never get to a point where you will say it is enough: "I will never get thirsty again." Accepting Christ means making a decision to follow the Lord's way of life and living like him on a permanent basis. It is a feeling of being thirsty for goodness and closeness to the love of God. It is a feeling of being insufficient by yourself, without anyone, or a superpower, who controls your life. The Samaritan woman says to Jesus, "Sir, give me this water so that I will not come here again to draw water . . ." (John 4:1–26). The taxman Zacchaeus says to the Lord Jesus, "Sir, have you seen, I will give fourfold of my possessions to the poor" (Luke 19:1–10). Nicodemus decided to approach the Lord Jesus at night to talk about his salvation and after being taught the method of receiving the Lord, he had to be born again (John 3:1–21). Isaiah had to be cleansed through a burning coal that wiped out his sin (Isa 6:1–11). Accepting Christ means to believe in God: that outside him there is no life eternal or satisfaction.

METHODS OF ACCEPTING THE LORD JESUS

1. *Accepting* in your heart, privately in your conscience, that you are a sinner and Jesus alone has come to rescue and save you from this sinful nature to renew your life permanently as a child of God. You may or may not be able to mark the date of such a decision to give your heart and life to Christ. But it's always an overwhelming turning point in life.
2. *Standing up*, openly and publicly pronouncing your decision to follow the Lord Jesus Christ is a way of boldly accepting Christ. You do this by surrendering all your life and its tribulations, successes, and failures. You can mark the date for this decision. It will always inspire you to move on in life with a sense of spiritual security.
3. *Realizing* a feeling of inadequacy and needing the Lord Jesus to lift you up for a better life full of renewal and spiritual security. This feeling of inadequacy and needing the Lord Jesus is a way of accepting the Lordship of Christ. This is the method which was manifest in the life of Nicodemus.
4. *Repenting* is saying to Christ 'I sinned in this particular way, but now I have changed my direction of doing wrong and I now desire a new lease of life." Paul says that if anyone is in Christ, he is a new creature; old things are gone and new life begins. Repentance creates a personal feeling of being forgiven by the Lord himself. The prodigal son felt this sense of guilt and came back to his senses once again.
5. *Responding* to the love of God, expressed by his generous gesture of sending his son to die for your sins. When you respond to his love you do so by accepting the Lordship of Jesus.

HOW DO YOU CONVINCE AN INDIVIDUAL TO ACCEPT CHRIST?

Step 1: Share with him the meaning of the love of God as shown in John 3.16. Share with the client the sinful nature of the human race through the first man Adam and how this has become our nature to sin and that God loved us to a point of giving us His son Jesus Christ as a salvation plan to redeem us from this fallen nature.

Step 2: Share with him the importance of preserving one's life to avoid remaining in this fallen nature, which results in eternal death and pain through perishing in one's sinful nature.

Step 3: Offer the client the Lord Jesus, to decide to believe in him. Convince the client that the Lord has a lot of spiritual, social, emotional, economic and personal interest, and space for him as an individual to be a child of God. Ask if he believes God is for us all. If yes, then God can save us all.

Step 4: Provide the client with the benefit of believing in God. The main benefit is that the client is saved from perishing.

Step 5: Share the importance of believing in God, that it will result in obtaining eternal (everlasting) life. This life is full of joy and spiritual protection.

Step 6: If the person is a new convert, pray with him a prayer of acceptance and commitment to the Lord Jesus. Ask that person to repeat a prayer after you, or ask that individual to say out loud his own payer. If you want to ask the convert to say a prayer after you, such a prayer may be something like this: "Heavenly Father, I present myself before you as a sinner in need of forgiveness. I accept you as my personal Saviour and Lord from today onwards. I belong to you now and forever. Amen." Ask him to say his own prayers as often as possible. Reveal to him the importance of knowing that Christ forgives forever. It is important for the individual to say this, or his own prayer, because it marks the beginning of a new life in his spiritual journey. It may well be that each time he is tempted to sin he remembers these words. They can protect him from any desire to sin.

Step 7: Show the person from scripture why God has gone to all this trouble, not just to forgive our sin, but to defeat evil so that he is worthy to receive the glory due to him.

CONFESSION OF SIN

There is no Christian anywhere in the world who can claim perfection in all circumstances. We sin in the way we think, talk, and behave to ourselves, our neighbors, and to God. We, therefore, need to confess our sins every day of our lives. To confess is to say out loud our sins and ask for forgiveness from God. When we do not confess our sins, those sins will eat us to death. The Bible says "people who cover over (hide) their sins will not prosper. But if they confess and forsake them, they will receive mercy" (Prov 28:13). The Apostle Paul confesses, "Christ Jesus came into the world to save sinners—and I was the worst of them all" (1Tim 1:15). The Bible helps us by saying, "confess your sins to each other and pray for each other so that you may be healed" (Jas 5:16). In addition, we learn that: "But if we confess our sins to him, he is faithful and just to forgive us and to cleanse us from every wrong" (1 John 1:9).

LIVING A NEW LIFE IN CHRIST

When we have repented and confessed our sins, we then live a new life in him who saved us from sin. The Apostle Paul teaches us, as he did to the Colossian church (3:1–17), to live a new life worthy of our calling as follows:

1. Set your sights on the realities of heaven where Christ sits at God's right hand of honor.
2. Let heaven fill your thoughts and do not only think of earthly things.
3. You died when Christ died, and your real life is hidden with Christ.
4. Christ is your real life and you will share his glory when he is revealed to the world.
5. Avoid earthly desires of sin such as lust, lying, sexual immorality, impurity, idolatry, and greediness, which invite God's anger.
6. Avoid anger, rage, malicious behavior, slander, and dirty language.
7. Clothe yourself with tenderhearted mercy, kindness, humility, gentleness, and patience.
8. Forgive each other, love one another, be peaceful, and live in harmony.
9. Use Christ's words to teach and counsel each other.
10. Always be a representative of the Lord Jesus.
11. Foolish talk, obscene stories, and coarse jokes are not for you.
12. Do not let the sun go down while you are still angry (Eph 4:26).
13. Remember: "We are not fighting against people made of flesh and blood, but against the evil rulers and authorities of the unseen world, against those mighty powers of darkness who rule this world . . ." (Eph 6:12).

14. Pray at all times and on every occasion in the power of the Holy Spirit. Stay alert and be persistent in your prayers for all Christians everywhere (Eph 6:18).

GIVING ONE'S LIFE AND WEALTH TO CHRIST

The bible says, "Don't give reluctantly or in response to pressure. God loves a person who gives cheerfully. And God will generously provide all you need. Then you will always have everything you need and plenty left over to share with others" (2 Cor 9:8). It is notable that God will reward a cheerful giver without fail as we read, "Godly people give to the poor. Their good deeds will never be forgotten (2 Cor 9:9). It is true that through giving ". . . you will be enriched so that you can give even more generously" (2 Cor 9:11). Giving to the Lord should not be selfish or self-centered but it must be done to the glory of God.

MAKING DISCIPLESHIP REAL

By definition, the word disciple, "*mathetes*" in Greek, means one who learns instruction from another.[1] The disciples of the Lord Jesus were people who were following and learning from the Lord. For a period of three years they worked with him. They were part of his ministry and mission. They healed the sick, taught the crowds, and prayed with the worshipping community of the day. A Christian disciple is one who is determined to follow Jesus Christ, with the desire to learn from him and live according to his example. "Therefore if anyone is in Christ, he is a new creation; the old has gone, the new has come" (2 Cor 5:17). To disciple is to make someone a Christian learner or apprentice, to train in the Christian life.[2] It involves baptizing and teaching people to obey everything Jesus teaches us. A disciple is an apprentice to a master, a craftsman, learning his particular trade, following his teaching, an adherent of his method, imitating his approach.[3] But the most important thing to remember in being a disciple of the Lord Jesus Christ is having a personal attachment with the Lord. This then shapes our inner life and behavior. This personal attachment to the Lord was a vital feature of the disciples. It means they were obedient to the Lord. A person may

1 Gordon, *Foundations of Christian Living*, 7.

2. White, *Effective Pastor*, 120.

3. Ibid.

not be able to tell the exact time and place, or trace all the chain of circumstances in the process of conversion; but this does not prove him to be unconverted.[4] This happened to Nicodemus, and Christ noticed it in him. He said, "The wind blows wherever it pleases. You hear its sound, but you cannot tell where it comes from or where it is going. So it is with everyone born of the Spirit." That regenerating power, which no human power, which no human eye can see, begets a new life in the soul; it creates a new being in the image of God.[5] While the work of the Holy Spirit is imperceptible, its effects are manifest.[6] If the heart has been renewed by the Holy Spirit, the life will bear witness to the fact. A change in our character, habits, and pursuits will show that we are disciples of the Lord Jesus. When we become his disciples we long to bear his image, breathe his Spirit, do his will, and please him in all things. All those who become new creatures in Christ will show fruits of the Spirit such as love, joy, peace, faith, gentleness, meekness, goodness, and patience—as reflected in Paul's letter to the Galatians. (5:22, 23). In addition we learn that we do not earn salvation by our obedience, for salvation is the free gift of God, to be received by faith.

MAJOR STEPS IN FULFILLING THE GREAT COMMISSION[7]

1. *Praying*: we pray for opportunities for the gospel to be preached and for protection for those who work for the Lord in witnessing (Col 4:3; Rom 15:30–31; Acts 4:29–31; Matt 9:38).
2. *Giving:* we give our finances and offer ourselves (2 Cor 8:1–4).
3. *Going:* the Lord didn't commission us to stay and wait for the world to come to us, but for us to go into the world to reach out to many (Matt 28:18–20). More than half the world population has never heard the gospel,[8] and it is a challenge to go out and reach them. True discipleship involves fulfilling the great commission.[9]

4 White, *Steps to Christ*, 3.

5. Ibid.

6. Ibid., 3.

7. Ibid., 251.

8. Gordon, *Foundations of Christian Living*, 252.

9. Ibid.

PRIVILEGES OF A DISCIPLE[10]

1. Chosen by God himself (Eph 1:4–5).
2. Christ is his personal Savior, who has forgiven his sins, making him acceptable to God (Rom 5.8).
3. He is a child of God (Gal 6:7).
4. He has been given eternal life (John 3:16).
5. The Holy Spirit lives in him, giving him power to witness (Acts 1:8).
6. Nothing can separate him from the love of God (Rom 8:38–39).

SPIRITUAL BENEFITS OF BEING A DISCIPLE[11]

1. Changes one's attitude towards people, money, business practices, and social responsibility.
2. Experiences a refining or purifying of one's life to an extent that one's attitude and actions, which may be inconsistent with the Lord, will be removed.
3. When you desire to act like Christ, he hears.
4. Love will govern your actions, words, attitudes, thoughts, and life.
5. You will become compassionate and willing to forgive.
6. You will inherit everything from God that Jesus inherits.
7. Changes for the better in your life will take place because the lord wants to see those changes in you (Col 3:17).
8. God will provide all your needs (Matt 6:3).

HOW DO YOU MAKE DISCIPLES?

1. Personal witnessing at individual level.
2. Group witnessing in the community or at the workplace.
3. Spiritual revivals for reviving members or gaining new ones.
4. Spiritual crusades with target groups or clients.
5. One-to-one evangelism, visiting people at the work place or in their homes.
6. Print media advertisements including newspapers.
7. Electronic media advertisements including television.
8. Hospital chaplaincy.
9. Army, prison, and police chaplaincy services.

10. Ibid. 4.
11. Ibid.

SIGNS OF SPIRITUAL MATURITY[12]

1. Fruitfulness in our service to God (Matt 25: 14–30).
2. Humble attitude and willingness to serve others (John 13: 12–17).
3. A standard of excellence in our lives (2 Cor 13:11).
4. Close relationship with Jesus (Gal 2:20).
5. Fruit of the Spirit manifests in our lives (Gal 5:22–23).
6. Stable, consistent, and holy walk before God and human kind (Eph 4:11–16).
7. Solid knowledge of God's word and discernment as a result (Heb 5:13).

COST OF DISCIPLESHIP?

1. Loss of friends.
2. Loss of relatives and property.
3. Being misunderstood.
4. Being blamed sometimes for something not genuine.
5. Being hated as you rebuke sinful lives.
6. Insufficient resources.
7. Working more hours for less remuneration.

HOW DO YOU CHOOSE SOMEONE TO DISCIPLE?

1. Find those who are prepared to listen.
2. Find those who are willing to learn.
3. Find those who are willing to forgive.
4. Find those who are willing to trust.
5. Find those who are willing to serve.
6. Find those who are willing to sacrifice.
7. Find those who are willing to love God and do the will of God.
8. Find those who are willing to admit their needs.

AIMS FOR MAKING DISCIPLES:[13]

1. To love God first and foremost (Matt 22:37).
2. To love one's neighbors as oneself (Matt 22:39).
3. To be transformed so as to become like the Lord himself (2 Cor 2:18).
4. To delight oneself in obeying God (John 14:21).

12. Ibid., 7.

13. Ibid., 268.

5. To grow in knowledge of the word of God through group teaching and discussion as well as personal Bible study (Luke 24:45).
6. To change one's lifestyle so that one dislikes things that dishonor God.
7. To learn so that one becomes more able in the skills of discipleship such as confidence, leading Bible study, testimony, teaching others to pray, and receiving the Holy Spirit (2 Tim 2:15).

EFFECTIVE METHODS OF SOUL WINNING:[14]

1. Get to know Jesus better (Phil 3:10).
2. Follow Jesus more closely by following five keys for effective fishermen:
    a) have a clear purpose, b) prepare carefully, c) know the place well, d) conceal your personality while raising the personality of Jesus, and e) be patient.
3. Uplift Jesus with your life, action, and word (John 12:32).

PASTOR' ROLE IN DISCIPLE-MAKING

In Paul's letter to the church in Ephesus (Eph 4:11–16) there is mention of general principles of pastoral practice. Four main functions have been noted: apostles, prophets, evangelists, and pastors/teachers. Apostles and prophets were foundational to the founding of the church (Eph 2:20). The apostles and prophets planted and shaped the early church, and today the work of outreach is done by evangelists.[15] The prophets taught the word and now that is done by teachers or pastors.[16]

THE DISCIPLE-MAKING PASTOR HAS FOUR MAJOR COMMITMENTS TO MAKE[17]

a) Place disciple-making at the heart of the church
b) Have a clear identification and communication of the role of the pastor, the people, and the disciple-making process
c) Make the priesthood of all believers
d) Multiply the membership (go and bear fruit, John 15:8, 16).

14. Gordon, *Foundations of Christian Living*, 260.
15. Ibid.
16. Ibid., 117.
17. Hull, *Disciple-Making Pastor*, 84.

Prayer: Dear God, please listen to the way I talk, pay attention to my deeds, mend my thoughts, and let these call others to serve you. Touch my lips and cleanse them, train my ears to hear your language, focus my eyes to see your image in other people. Amen.

5

Spiritual Formation

MEANING OF SPIRITUAL FORMATION?

THE TERM *SPIRITUAL FORMATION* refers to spiritual transformation, renewal, restoration, and reorientation of oneself. It is a process of experiencing the grace of God in a new form. It is accessing the grace of God in a new pattern. It is a new walk with God and a new realization of the fact that God is part of us as his children and we are part of him as his children. It is a special way of being formed into a new child of God. Spiritual formation is a rebirth of lost brotherhood and sisterhood in Christ. It is a renewed companionship with Christ at a time when we need him most because of our fallen state.

Others define spiritual formation as the progressive patterning of a person's inner and outer life according to the image of Christ through intentional means of spiritual growth.[1] Spiritual formation can also be understood as the process whereby God is transforming the believers' life and character towards the life and character of the Lord Jesus Christ.[2] It involves God transforming people into the image of his son Jesus Christ. Spiritual formation means that God is in the business of forming us into his likeness so that we can have a deeper fellowship with him and reflect the virtues of righteousness in our lives.[3] It also involves change which is brought into our lives through the power of God's grace. It derives from the Holy Spirit in the context of forming, transforming or conforming (from) a person's life toward Christlikeness (until Christ is formed in us, Gal 4:19b, Rom 12:1–2, 2 Cor. 3:17–18).

1 Lawrence, *Dynamics of Spiritual Formation*, 15.

2. Pettit, *Foundations of Spiritual Formation*, 24.

3. Ibid.

METHODS OF SPIRITUAL FORMATION

1. Personal prayer
2. Personal meditation
3. Personal fasting
4. Personal bible study as a way of talking to God and listening to him as he instructs us to be like Christ in our daily lives
5. Fellowship with Christ and other people
6. Personal devotion by devoting a special time for entering into a conversation with the Lord
7. Tithing as a way of personal communication with the Lord in a special way
8. Retreating from usual business to find time alone with the Lord
9. Class meetings with other Christians
10. Regular family devotion
11. Personal relationship with God

DISCIPLINE FOR SPIRITUAL FORMATION

The following are important ways in which we can enhance spiritual formation as a discipline. If we practice these spiritual disciplines, we move closer to the Lord each day of our lives in a special way.

1. Worship
2. Service
3. Scripture
4. Presence
5. Relationship
6. Belief
7. Faith
8. Obedience
9. Humility

METHODS OF INVITING JESUS CHRIST FOR PERSONAL CHANGE AND COMPANY

1. Abraham and his hospitality: (Gen 18).

When Abraham and Sarah received visitors in their home, they realized later that they had invited God himself into their family. In turn God rewarded their hospitality by giving a gift for which their hearts had always longed: a baby boy. When we invite God into our lives we receive the best of what he can offer to us through his son Jesus Christ.

2. **The Shunamite woman and her wealth: "Let us make a little chamber, and let us set for him there a bed, and a table, and a stool, and a candle stick" (2 Kgs 4:8–36).**

The Sunammite woman who gave the man of God, Elisha, a high form of hospitality was also given a child for whom she and her husband had longed to have for many years. The child came at an appropriate time after God saw her commitment to serving the man of God. When the child died she invited Elisha into the situation. The prophet Elisha prayed for the child and the child's life was restored. When we invite God into our homes and situations great changes in challenging situations happen to us as a result of such invitation of God.

3. **Zaccheus, the hated provides hospitality to the Lord: "Today salvation has come to this house" (Luke 19:9).**

This man had been a tax collector who cheated many people by collecting more than what was required for the government. But when he made an effort to see Jesus by climbing onto a tree, Jesus came into his life and home. Immediately there was change in his thinking and perception of other people. He says to the Lord "I will give to the poor fourfold."

4. **The Samaritan woman at the well: "Come, see a man who told me all that I have done." (John 4:29).**

The Samaritan woman who met with Jesus at the well found that the Lord could bring her salvation and everlasting life. When we converse with Jesus we experience everlasting life. There is nothing else that will supersede Christ in our lives.

5. **Nicodemus by night: (John 3:1–36).**

The man who visited the Lord by night was Nicodemus. He got the attention he needed and received salvation, thereby seeking company with Christ. When we seek the company of the Lord any time we will find him, as he has time for each one of us regardless of our social status. We may be poor or rich; the Lord has time for us to listen to our concerns, sorrows, and joys, as well. We suffer with him and celebrate with him; all the time we need his presence.

6. **Cleopas and his friend on the road to Emmaus: "Lord, abide with us" (Luke 24:29).**

The Lord joined Cleopas and his colleague on the road to Emmaus. As evening drew close they invited Jesus to stay with them for the night. The Lord agreed. As they had dinner together, they learned more about the greatness of the Lord's presence among them. When we invite Christ into our homes and lives, we experience a newness of life brought about by his presence.

7. **Mary and Martha, and the loss of their brother Lazarus: "Lord, come and see" (John 11:34).**

Both women always invited Jesus into their home. But in this particular incident they invited him to see the resting place, or grave, of their brother, even though they had earlier provided hospitality to him in a special way. "Where have you put him?" Jesus asked. "Come and see," they said. At the death of their brother Lazarus, the Lord came and made a difference in their lives by bringing their beloved brother back to life. When Jesus enters into our situations we experience miracles, changes of situations, and our hopes and aspirations are fulfilled. The Lord is the source of our hope. But do you always know who to invite into your problems? Other people make them worse. Others cause more pain and suffering. But the Lord makes problems lighter. Invite him now! He transforms your situation with a difference.

8. **The Gentile Woman: "Come to me all who are heavy laden, I will give you rest" (Matt 11:28).**

Even dogs deserve God's attention, the Gentile woman insisted in her mind when she sought the attention of the Lord Jesus. Her daughter was sick. She knew where to get assistance. She invited Jesus into her situation. The invitation made a difference. It is always important to know where to get assistance when things go wrong in our lives. Christ has the solutions to our inner and most complicated challenges of life. At some stage he says, "come to me all who are heavy laden, I will give you rest." He has a passion for our problems. When he decides to address them, his solutions are final. He forms change in our situations.

9. **Jesus at a wedding: (John 2:1–12).**

The Lord attended a wedding at Cana. He was invited as a guest. A precious commodity of the wedding (wine) ran out. The steward in charge of the wedding was given instructions to help the situation. The Lord's mother gave the steward important advice that changed a crisis of wine shortage to a restoration of all when she told him to talk to Jesus and said, "do everything he tells you" (John 2:5).

JUNIOR CHURCH SPIRITUAL FORMATION

The junior church is one of the most important pillars of the church for all centuries. God's salvation has come into the world through a child, Emmanuel (Isa 7:14). The bible says "train a child in the way he should go, and when he is old he will not turn from it" (Prov 22:6). The Lord Jesus had a passion for children. He says, "let them come to me . . ." Without the junior church, the current church has no future. So, it is important for any congregation to develop the junior church in a significant way. Ask children to sing in church every Sunday or ask them to read the bible or recite bible verses before the start of the worship service or ask them to sing in groups or individually. Ask them to choose their own leaders and say how they feel they would like to participate in church activities. This is forming Christ in them. By the time they become adults, spiritually they are already formed. Some of the ways in which the junior church can be spiritually formed are listed below:

1. Developing self-esteem: help them to believe in themselves and in God, helping them to be the best of all children God has made on earth.
2. Developing talent: identify what they are able to do for the church and for themselves and let them express that in the best way they can in church.
3. Developing confidence: ask them to do important tasks in the church.
4. Raising preachers in children: have a preaching schedule for the worship service.
5. Raising leaders in children: help them elect leaders among themselves for tasks in the church.

6. Role modeling children: help them identify people in society they feel are role models. They must give reasons why they feel such persons are good role models.
7. Teaching children to study the bible: help children conduct bible study beginning with a few verses.
8. Teaching children to sing in church: every Sunday the junior church must sing in church. This is great spiritual formation.
9. Teaching children the ministry of charity: help them to identify needy people for them to care for socially. When they become adults they are already responsible.
10. Teaching children to support the church: help them to support the church in a way that they themselves identify.
11. Motivating children to love God: help them understand the meaning of love as given to us by God our Father through the coming of Christ into the world (John 3:16).
12. Teaching children to love the church: help them to understand the role of the church by asking them what they think the church stands for and discussing their answers.

6

Managing People with Passion

WHAT IS THE MEANING OF PASSION?

THE WORD *PASSION* IN biblical perception means an inner feeling or sense of personal professional attachment to the flock. God feels this for us as his children. He has an eternal passion for us as part of his creation. We are sinners and yet redeemed by his saving grace. We plead for the Lord's mercy through his grace. The Lord Jesus always had a passion for the sick, outcasts, tax collectors, and the hated and despised of society. He felt "compassion" for those who could not walk, talk, hear, or see because of their condition of disability. He did not just see and then ignored them. He acted in order to save them from their disability and reduce or eliminate their pain. He has a great passion for those people in stressful conditions and under severe social pressure; He also experienced spiritual torment up until he was betrayed and put to death. He gave up his life for those in spiritual and physical poverty to save them from their pitiful situations. He died like a criminal to save criminals from their sinful state. His arms and feet pierced with nails to save human kind. It was an act of love and compassion. Prior to this the way towards the cross was all pain and suffering. All this is meant to save humanity from the bondage of sin.

Today those who follow in the footsteps of Christ as disciples, such as pastors, must have a passion for the ministry, or for the church, and the people they lead. As pastors, we go through difficult times in the work of the church and yet we must persevere in the great task to save human kind from the wrath of sin and death, from physical and spiritual disability of many types. We must lead the church, God's people, with passion. For the sake of the church, the gospel, the Lord's work, many leaders in the church today have been spitted upon, ridiculed, given all sorts of names and stripped of their professional integrity and dignity, but this must even inspire us to have greater passion for the church of God from one glory to another. There is never a time when the church is wealthy and without need. Neither has it ever been without the poor within it. Jesus even says "you always have the poor among you," but he had passion for all. This is the pattern of leadership that today's pastor must have. Have a strong sense to care for everyone, rich or poor.

On the other hand, the people themselves would want to do the best for the church in terms of support but they are suffering and in pain and under stress to make the church, the word of God, the people of God, live forever in the life to come. Under these circumstances the church must be administered with a great sense of passion. You administer the church while both you and it are in pain for survival, sustenance, and moral uprightness. Evil, corruption, bribes, prostitution, theft, murder, and terrorism are at their worst in the world today—human life is under physical and spiritual threat of permanent life in hell. But this is the world where the church is living and working. This is the world, of which the church must transform and not be transformed by. It is an uphill task but it must be accomplished through the guidance of the Holy Spirit.

One of the most taxing difficulties of our time is providing pastoral care to the human soul, mind, and body. The image of God is reflected in this setup. Property, movable or immovable, is easier to manage because the response controls are fairly administrable. Humanity is complex to manage partly because of the combination of sinfulness and purity reflected in the flesh and soul. What the human mind ponders on is a mystery. It's a combination of saintly thoughts, spiritually uplifting ambitions, and inspiring hopes on the one hand, and a sense of rubbish, evil, and horrible flesh (St. Paul found that his mind would do what he did not wish it to do even if he knew what would be good to do). For this reason people management is both difficult and complex. So, to manage people you need patience. Not only that, you need love, empathy, and compassion that must be overwhelming. Short of that you manage them the way a businessperson manages his tomatoes or goats or machines that have no soul. No matter how difficult or incorrigible they may become, no matter how insincere, untruthful, hateful, no matter how hurt you may be, just remember that they are human and they deserve to be treated with a sense of passion—just like Christ always had for many of those whom he came across: for instance, the Samaritan woman; Nicodemus; Zaccheaus, the dreamer; Joseph; the adulterer David who took Bathsheba Uriah's wife; the Prophet Isaiah; Jeremiah; or the man that saw the burning bush, Moses. All of them had their weaknesses and problems, but God has always had a passion for them. And for that reason the birth of the church through the resurrection of Christ has come into being to represent God's presence in humanity. If all people were perfect, good, truthful, pure in heart, and God-fearing would we need a church? But to get us back into a positive relationship God the church tries to remind us every day that the blood of Jesus shed on the cross has set us free once again to join the forgiven community of faith, called Christians. We, then, must be administered into this relationship through God's representatives on earth and in the church whose passion heralds the unending grace of God.

Managing people with compassion in the church means that the pastor must create special time with the people that he leads. Take time to learn from them. Take an audit of what their perceptions about you are as a leader. If you are a manager, take time to relate and talk to the least known person at the church. Take time to talk to the groundsmen. Or have a chat with the tea boy or the woman who sweeps the floor. Ask them what they think about the church or management. Ask them what people say about you. This must also happen at a higher level where the chief executive works with a core group of directors.

The pastor needs to take special informal time to also mix and talk to the people who are not leaders in the church. Take time to listen to what they have to say about your church or congregation. At the denominational level ask them what they understand about you as the pastor of the church. It will be amazing to know what they think about you. If we fear being told the negative truths about ourselves, then that means we have areas that need to be improved upon in our administration of the church. A good leader must want to learn from his mistakes. Meeting and talking to people that you lead informally is one of the excellent methods of creating lasting closeness and relations with colleagues in the church or any other organization. Poor administrators of the church isolate themselves from the ordinary people they lead. The gap creates space for gossip and speculation, which leads to the leader's isolation and unpopularity.

ACCEPT EVERY PERSON AS DIFFERENT

It is a theological truth that God created each one of us different from one another. Even twin children can never be the same in terms of interests, emotions, feelings, attitudes, strengths and weaknesses, as well as capabilities and talents. What each one of us likes or dislikes or what each one of us considers to be important is not the same all the time. This is critical for any church leader or administrator of any organization to know at every level. Therefore, it is an unfortunate mistake if the pastor compares members and leaders of his congregation to each other assuming they could be the same.

A good administrator must have the ability to identify the talent of each of the people he leads and apportion recognition and praise accordingly. Some people say it's a skill or an art of administration to be able to do that. Others say it's just professional knack to be able to identify the small good things that people do and then reward them appropriately. Yet others say it is a gift to be able to recognize a good deed from a person who is very unpopular or is known to be very critical or even willful all the time. It is naturally very difficult to get some people to see positive aspects of any debate or issues under discussion. Other people do not weigh the facts; they put the weight on the person who has made that contribution. So, they do not respond to the debate or question on the table but to the person who has said something. Other people oppose everything if it comes from the leader. If the same thing is said by a different person, they will accept it with no reservation. A good leader must accommodate all these types of people and treat as different as they are.

There are many leaders in the church today who do not accept criticism. They feel uncomfortable when criticized in public or in private. They say that this will affect them spiritually. Others say it's stressful. Other leaders do not even give a chance to those they know to be their opponents because they are not sure what will come out of their opponents' mouths. It is vital to know that criticism, whether negative or constructive; it is good for any leader in the church or any organization. It keeps you on your toes. It has never killed anyone. It improves your skills as a leader especially the way you relate to those that do not call you "sir" all the time. Further, criticism of any type makes you grow spiritually. Those that criticize you provide a ladder for you on which to step over their heads to greater heights in your administration. When they criticize you they make you a better leader. Criticism is a source of administrative strength. Those who fear it lose out! Those who accept it learn something out of it. By the way, you can be criticized for doing well. And as the Bible puts it, all works well for the good of those who love the Lord.

At best, every individual deserves the right to be praised if he has done well. Make it a habit to appreciate other people and to give them credit just the way you would want other people to appreciate your achievement. Most people feel better if their achievements are recognized and rewarded.

LOVE THEM ALL

In the Lord's perception of life the greatest commandment is love. In his ethical teaching, Jesus instructs all of us to love one another as he has loved all of us. He said the same thing to his disciples. But most important, he gave us a very difficult task, which perhaps ninety percent of us as Christians fail to abide by. This is the challenge to love our enemies. And yet this is a great test of our work and life as disciples of the Lord Jesus. Today it is not surprising that two thirds of all leaders in the church hate people they perceive to be their enemies.

There is always something that happens when a leader loves all the people he leads. People will understand you better.

a) Always tell the truth. Telling the truth is a gift from God. Not many people have this gift. If telling the truth is a hard thing for you, pray about it.
b) Be fair and firm when dealing with issues of an administrative nature or anything to do with human feelings.
c) Avoid talking ill of other people. See every person as having potential to do good in their circumstances.
d) Do not get excited about other people's mistakes. Be prepared to help them out.
e) Avoid despising other people who may be less privileged or talented. Do not have a low opinion of them.
f) Accept people as they are, not as you wish they could be. God created them as they are, not as you wish they could be. If they do things you disagree with or never like, then pray for God to effect change.
g) Apologize to them as subordinates when you make a mistake. Don't be bossy.

MEDITATION

One of the strongest ways in which an administrator for any church lives up to a continual relationship with God is through meditation. Meditation means being in communication with God without having to show many people what is going on between you and your God. We learn that there were many people in the Bible whose meditation made a difference in their lives and the lives of many other people. Through meditation, Christ makes changes in the lives of humankind. For example, Nicodemus went to see the Lord about his spiritual life after undergoing personal meditation. The Lord said to him that he must be born again for him to attain everlasting life. Similarly, from meditating, Zacchaeus made a plan to see Jesus by climbing onto a sycamore tree. It worked because when Jesus came to where Zacchaeus was, the tax collector asked Jesus to go with him to his house. It was when the Lord was received into the tax collector's house that Zacchaeus received salvation. In his own words Jesus said, "Today salvation has come into this house." Personal salvation comes through meditation. On another occasion, the woman of Samaria meditated about her spiritual life when she was in a discussion with Jesus at the well of Jacob. Towards the end of the conversation she says to Jesus, "Sir, let me have this water so that I will not come back here to fetch water again." Meditation brings about a new lease of spiritual life.

DELEGATION

Delegation is an art of administration. It is an instance where a leader extends his responsibility to a subordinate to carry out set goals on his behalf. It is a gift to be able to know who, among the people you lead, gets things done the best way. Very good leaders do this and then follow up with their subordinates to review progress on set targets. To delegate does not mean to abandon, although it is known in the modern world that the laziest leaders of our time get things accomplished by using other people, while they get paid for doing nothing. But they have a certain trick they use. When things go well they want the credit. When things go wrong they blame the person they have delegated. Delegation is not about off-loading, or dumping, mundane and unwanted tasks on team members or other people.[1] It is a process by which a leader provides

1 Chalke and Relph. *Making a Team Work*, 72.

team members an opportunity to develop new skills, handle responsibility, gain confidence, and therefore achieve success.[2] The word *delegate* could be interpreted to mean the following:

D=decide what to delegate

E=elect who to delegate

L=list what's involved

E=explain the task

G=give adequate training

A=allow freedom to work

T=tell others about the delegation

E=evaluate performance.[3]

Most leaders delegate and forget to follow up on progress. This is the stage where most leaders fail or make a difference. Some subordinates who know that their leader is forgetful exploit them in a miserable way. To avoid being exploited by subordinates when you delegate responsibilities to them, choose someone who will not destabilize your work; find someone with talent and potential skill to benefit from the task, or one who would like to take the challenge.[4] And then jot down in your note book who has been delegated to do what, how, and by when the results of the task should be reported back. Good leaders everywhere in the world work with deadlines that help them achieve desired goals by a given period. Poor leaders leave tasks hanging in the air. Very poor leaders delegate and forget all about what they have delegated. No matter how excellent your subordinate is, you need a method to check progress on what you have delegated. Some leaders pretend to be very busy and have no time to follow up on whether the tasks they have delegated are being done.

In the Bible (Exod18:1–27) Jethro advised his son-in-law Moses to apply this administrative theory of delegation. It worked for him because it gave him time to rest and refresh so that he no longer needed to spend the whole day trying cases that needed his attention. Delegation gives you time to enjoy leadership because you do not have all the activi-

2. Ibid.

3. Ibid.

4. Ibid.

ties centered on you. This is healthy for any administrator as it reduces stress. Leaders who try to do everything themselves most of the time, do less in terms of quality.

In terms of their role at the local church, the pastor must not leave everything to the lay leader or finance committee because if the pastor leaves this congregation, the next pastor will find it very hard to control such a congregation. The pastor's role is to lead the congregation. The pastor must never take a back seat in the name of delegation to cover for laziness, especially in terms of preaching and teaching the word of God. If for some special reason the pastor has to delegate a lay preacher to preach or teach the word of God, the pastor must be present or make a follow up of what has been preached or taught for the good of the congregation. Be jealous of your pulpit.

Some pastors have no idea, or don't care, what food their flock will be fed, and by whom and at what stage of its spiritual level. The pastor is a member of all the committees in order to give pastoral guidance and advice and to know what is going on in every committee. There is no committee above the pastor in most denominations. At the same time, the pastor is not a dictator; he is there as an ex-officio member of all the committees in order to stabilize debate, control emotions, and help the leaders of the committees maintain a clear focus on the mission of the church and of that particular congregation. The pastor must be firm and fair and help church leaders of his congregation to operate within the values of this framework. It is good for the church to function in a good, friendly, and gentle social and spiritual atmosphere.

ATTITUDE

Attitude is the way a person views something or someone or oneself. A person can look at an individual and create an opinion that is negative or positive about that particular human being. The pastor can develop an opinion on certain individuals in the church depending on whether he, the pastor, feels they are worthy or not by human standards. Whichever way you define attitude towards certain individuals in the church, think positively about other people. Have a positive image of God in God's people. Some might drift away and blur the image of God in themselves; ignore that and concentrate on the good. A positive attitude towards people makes life easy for you as the pastor because you can hardly develop hate towards God's image. Neither would you like God to develop that same negative attitude towards you. People are a creation of God; they can never be substituted for anything else. They are in the image of God and that is a permanent principle of life. So what must change is the way you look at them. There are many advantages for always having a positive attitude towards other people in life. The main advantage is that you will always be a free person, whether you are alone or with other people. If other people have a negative attitude towards you, be positive about their negativity. Some people call this spiritual maturity. In the church and in the Bible this means to walk an extra mile when somebody asks you to walk one mile or giving the other cheek when you are beaten on one.

Another advantage of always having a positive attitude towards anyone or anything is that you are always successful, even before you start on anything or any tasks. A negative attitude towards a task or challenge is one sure way of failing to get off the ground. Candidates fail examinations before they even sit for them because they have a negative attitude towards their teachers and the material they are supposed to study. As a pastor, have a positive attitude towards your leaders and members of your congregation, even those you feel make life uncomfortable for you. This principle applies for every person who is in any administrative position in the church or any organization. In administration attitude can be your best friend or your worst enemy because it can it can motivate or demotivate you in your work.

Prayer: Almighty God, please inspire me to lead your people with a passion to do good. Assist my spirit to appreciate my weaknesses and turn them into sources of strength. Guide my ways and my conscience. Deliver me from selfishness. Amen.

7

Leadership Development

WHAT IS LEADERSHIP DEVELOPMENT?

How do you develop leaders for the church in order to realize its mission and ministry? Steps must be taken to train, teach, orient, build confidence, and trust in the leaders. Another key aspect of developing leaders is to love them. Loving one another is one of the most valuable tools the Lord Jesus used in his ministry of leadership with his disciples. He loved them. They loved him, too. For that reason, they developed credible confidence in each other. Their work became positively challenging and expanded throughout the world.

Leadership development refers to any deliberate effort by any organization to grow its personnel resource base. There is no one in the world who can claim to be born a leader. All leaders grow into leading. It is possible, though, to talk of talented leaders, but they are never born with their leadership abilities. God has provided each leader with a desire to lead. It is this desire that organizations bank on if they have to develop any sound leadership for their enterprise. To excel in any leadership position in the world there are basic ingredients that are pertinent. These are motivation, confidence, attitude, and integrity. These can be built in a person over time and experience. All good, sound leaders are found to have one or more of these ingredients.

The church needs people with such ingredients for its various levels of spiritual work. Our Lord Jesus was very particular in his choice of leaders, those who became his disciples. He chose people who were doing something at the time of their calling. The church must never choose people who are not doing anything for its leadership positions. Choosing people who are doing nothing to do God's work is dangerous because it is likely that such people will continue to do nothing for the church.

WHAT TYPE OF LEADERS DO YOU CHOOSE?

Every church has a polity of choosing leaders. In some denominations leaders are elected based on given guidelines. In others a nominations committee first sits to perform a preliminary selection, from which the entire congregation will then choose its final list of leaders. The bible gives an example of what type of leaders could be chosen in terms of quality. They must be trustworthy, reliable, and well mannered. This is important because other people in the church must find good examples of leadership in them. Among several types of leaders a congregation can choose are those with some or all of these qualities:

1. Reliable in all circumstances so that everyone can depend on them.
2. Respectful to all members of the church and community.
3. Kind in all respects to all members of the church and community.
4. Loving to all children of God within and outside of church.
5. Accommodative to all members despite their social status in the church and society.
6. Honest in thinking and action for the good of the church—not found to be serving personal interest.
7. Supportive to all other leaders and members.
8. Slow to anger and patient.
9. Solution-oriented and not always fault-finding.

HOW DO YOU CHOOSE LEADERS?

The method of choosing leaders for any congregation is an important exercise for any church. What makes it important is the fact that it may affect relations within the congregation. Further, if a mistake is made in the choice of leadership, the congregation suffers until the next election. The following steps may be taken in this important exercise:

1. Pray for the Lord to show you the best leadership, which the congregation deserves. Remember what the Lord Jesus did before choosing the disciples. He prayed all night.

2. Consult with some of the most reliable members of the congregation. Consultation here means talking with the members and asking them who they think could be suitable leaders for the positions you are proposing. Ask them why they prefer some people and not others.

Consult the most critical, the most reserved, and the most difficult members on who they think can take certain positions in leadership. Take personal time to think and pray about the names that have been suggested.

3. Advise the congregation of the exercise in time for them to make informed decisions about their own leadership.
4. Design a form that all members will fill out, to include one possible position they feel they can hold in that particular year.
5. On the day the nomination committee sits, produce the forms and ask the secretary of the committee to look through all of them and then give you an idea of how the positions can be filled. Ask the committee to make necessary adjustments depending on your knowledge of the general membership.
6. During the nomination committee sitting, give an orientation on the importance of confidentiality of the discussions and decisions to be taken.
7. When certain names are suggested and rejected, for personal or professional reasons, make sure the name is dropped with dignity regardless of the circumstances surrounding it because you and the congregation have a pastoral responsibility to that individual.
8. In the nomination committee meeting, keep the discussion at a professional, rather than personal, level. You may find that there are some members of the committee who have personal interests in some names or positions or others who may have been programmed to nominate certain names without meaningful reasons. That is normal in any election exercise. The best thing to do is to have an ability to manage the situation in the best interest of the church.
9. Be fair, firm, and honest when discussing peoples' names for leadership. If the exercise produces good results, the congregation will rejoice. If it fails, you are responsible. So, you are accountable either way.

10. On the day of the election, set a free atmosphere. Usually the congregation may have some tension or electoral fever or discomfort as most may be anxious about who will be elected for each position. Others fear losing some of the positions that they or their friends or relatives currently have.
11. When a name is given in addition to the list of those already nominated and you are aware that such a name has been dropped during the nomination committee meeting for moral or other confidential reasons, be bold to advise the congregation without explaining the circumstances surrounding such a name. Find a diplomatic and honorable way to ask the congregation to drop the name without humiliating the individual nominee. This is professional ethics. Never allow the congregation to make a mistake that will cost you or the congregation an embarrassment for which a correction will be difficult to consider afterwards.

WHEN DO YOU CHOOSE LEADERS?

In some churches a stipulation is made as to how many years one can serve in one position. If there is no regulation guiding this principle, the congregation can advise you ahead of time. The general advice, however, in all circumstances is that it is not a good idea to have one leader serve in one position for many years. This will not give other people a chance to lead the church. It is often notable that congregations that change its leaders at appropriate times perform better as new talent brings in new ideas for the good of the church. Congregations that reshuffle leaders periodically have a chance to experience new ideas. However, some congregations have a problem of recycling the same leaders in a few positions all the time. It is important to change leadership for the sake of injecting new blood in some idle committees.

Change must not be abrupt unless there is a problem. Committees deserve to be given time to excel in their work. Change must not be influenced by hate, grudge, or gossip. All these damage the church if they influence change in leadership. Change management must be a prayerful exercise. It must not be emotionally charged. Rather, it must be spiritually and professionally motivated. The congregation itself must say when change is due. However, you as the leader may feel there is need for change in some offices. If you feel this way, a lot of care in managing such change is called for. Share your feeling for the need for a change with your leaders. They will advise you accordingly. Or, alternatively, share this idea with your supervisor and provide honest reasons why you feel this way.

HOW DoYOU EMPOWER YOUR LEADERS?

The following are some of the ways you can empower your leaders after they are sworn into office:

1. Organize a spiritual retreat with them for an orientation, away from the rest.
2. Train them on what is expected of them.
3. Teach them to respect their responsibilities and their committee members.
4. Provide a detailed written list of their responsibilities and give a copy to each one.
5. Give each one an opportunity to read out the responsibilities and provide them a chance to say if they cannot understand some or all their tasks as given on the list.
6. Build their confidence and capacity for leadership by providing them with a clear reporting system.
7. Give them parameters of supervision.
8. Build trust in them.
9. Give the freedom of access to share if there are any problems in the committee.
10. Leave communication channels open for this sharing, on positive or negative developments.

HOW DO YOU EVALUATE THEIR EFFECTIVENESS?

Evaluation here refers to a regular check for progress in the work of the leaders. The following mechanism can be put in place to check progress on each committee:

1. Set dates for committee meetings without fail.
2. Provide guidelines for checking.
3. Every meeting must have minutes of the previous deliberations.
4. The minutes must carry the following items: Name of church; date, time, and venue of previous meeting; list of members present at that meeting; apologies named; list of absentees; items discussed;

action taken on issues discussed; action items that were given and the names of people who were given such tasks; time of ending the meeting; date of next meeting; and the name of the person who gave the closing prayer. This is a management instrument for effective leaders.

5. Every official decision of the committee must be recorded and produced when reporting progress.
6. Follow-up tasks set in the previous meeting through persons identified.

DEVELOPING LEADERSHIP QUALITIES IN ADMINISTRATION

i. What are the qualities of good administration?

Good church administration qualities are not an art but a gift from God. A pastor with these qualities has, among others: strong character, charisma, commitment, communication skills, competence, courage, discernment, focus, generosity, initiative, listening abilities, passion, positive attitude, problem-solving skills, strong relationships, responsibility, security, self-discipline, servanthood, and vision.[1] To keep leading you must keep learning and to get ahead you must put others first.[2] Those that force themselves to be good administrators or leaders when they are not only manage to earn sympathy from the people they lead. They can get some things done properly, but they lack communication in two things: God's passion for people and a personal touch with human relations. Others have a special gift to work well with other people. Some are selfish. They want all good things to belong to them or be said about them while they cannot say anything good about other people. This is not a sign of good leadership. They want all the glory and not have any of it go to other people.

A good administrator must not behave this way. He must know his functions well for it is from these that his efficiency and success can be measured. He must be fair and firm, passionate and considerate, principled and accountable. This means that he must stand for his ideals and

1. For a detailed discussion of the qualities of a leader, see Maxwell, *The 21 Indispensable Qualities of a Leader.*

2. Ibid., vi.

convictions. It means that he can explain himself clearly and consistently if required to do so.

As a leader, when you make a statement you must feel comfortable repeating it to other people, even many times, without feeling uncomfortable or ashamed of it. Also, you should be comfortable if other people say the same statement to you. As an administrator it is not a good habit to make life uncomfortable for the people you lead for any reason. If you feel they hate you for one reason or another, pray about it and then ask God to give you courage to talk to them privately about how you feel about what they said. Do not keep it to your self or pretend you are not hurt. Sharing helps you maintain a professional level of workmanship. Hiding it is dangerous because when you explode you lose the choice of words. Approach them when the anger has subsided and you develop a friendly language and choice of words.

As a leader you must know that naturally there are some people who are difficult or who just do not like anyone called a leader. Others just do not like your personality; you do not impress them at all. These people cannot be changed by your language or appeal. It may even be impossible to change them. Only God will help you to get along with them. Trying to change them will be both frustrating and a waste of time and energy. There are several reasons for such persons to behave the way they do. One reason for their natural hatred of leadership is the way they may have been brought up or the way they have arisen to their current positions. If they were brought up in a social environment where there were violent ways of drawing attention, they will always behave this way in public towards administration without being ashamed. If they rebuke leadership in public, this is the way they may have been brought up culturally, where an adult is never respected. You as a leader cannot change such people, but you can manage them. Others get angry and emotional very easily. You cannot change them. Others use very bad language. You cannot change them either. Others feel overjoyed when you are embarrassed. You cannot change their attitude to make them like you. All you can do is not behave like them. That is the difference between you and them. Maintain this distance. It protects you from sinking and stinking as an administrator. This happens whether you like it or not. If they lose their temper and you lose yours, too, or if they become emotional and you do the same, then you have failed to remain a leader. You will have lost control of your position as a leader. A leader must not always be predictable. You will be taken for granted or for a ride or both. When Jesus was arrested and accused of being the Son of God, he said, ". . . you say that I am." He did not say yes, which they were expecting to hear and ultimately crucify him for. Likewise, when the Pharisees asked him to whom they should pay taxes, Jesus did not meet their prediction and tell them to pay Caesar or do not pay taxes, which they were expecting to hear. But he dismissed them cleverly by asking them to give to Caesar what belongs to Caesar and to God what belongs to God.

A leader must not be emotional. Avoid such words as stupid, foolish, rubbish, nonsense, and rogue, even when you know very well that somebody is being exactly what that word describes. There is always a better language to express your unhappiness. Treat them as human because you know they are truly human, even when they have a different opinion from yours. In any case, you have no monopoly of opinion in the church. You are not God. You are only a leader who is in a position only for a period of time to facilitate a process of salvation for humankind through God's grace. The church was there before you and will be there for many more years after you will be gone. So, just participate by experiencing the grace of God in your time and add a brick to the building of the Kingdom of God and leave the rest to God himself.

Leadership or administration is service to the people of God not in your own way, but in God's way. Think the way God thinks, talk the way God talks, listen the way God listens, walk the way God walks, feel the way God feels, and look at things and people the way God looks at things and people. That is quality leadership. You view the world as God views it. That is the only way to appreciate a positive perception of the world in which we live. God would never have given us his son to die for our sins if he viewed the world with a negative attitude.

ii) What are the functions of an effective leader?[3]

a) Planning: There is no successful work that can be achieved by anyone without planning. All pastors must have time to sit down in an office and plan their work. Planning provides a framework to identify what needs to be done, when, why, how, and by whom.

b) Organizing: This involves ordering events into action plans and effectively making sure the work planned is done within a given frame-

3. Miller, *Leadership is the Key*, 92.

work. Who does what, in order to achieve what has been planned, is the function of organizing. What resources can be used to achieve desired results is all part of organizing.

c) Directing: This involves showing the congregation which direction the church must move. The pastor must not wait for the laity to show each other which direction the church must go. He must show the way. Direct events, trends, action, thinking, philosophy, perception, discussion, discourse, and speech for the church to remain focused.

d) Staffing: The pastor must help the congregation select effective and God-fearing members for positions of leadership. Where the congregation employs personnel for various staffing positions such as clerical staff, caretakers, treasurers, or accountants, the pastor must give advice and proper guidance in keeping with Christian ethics and expectations of the congregation. The selection process must be well planned, organized, ordered, transparent, and considerate.

e) Controlling: There must be adequate control of all activities going on at the church. Nothing must slip out of order in terms of planning, information sharing, and direction of events pertaining to the spiritual development of the congregation.

iii) What are leadership qualities in modern administration?

Below are listed qualities of a good administrator in the church, or in the secular world, that most leaders have confirmed as critical for sound management of both large and small organizations:

1. Accommodative: There are some people in the congregation who are less noticeable. But they contribute meaningfully to the life of the church. The pastor must make an effort to accommodate them in all programs. In addition, those who appear to be difficult would need to be accommodated into the life of the church. They must not be sidelined. Those who are difficult are in fact helping you to see things differently.

2. Trustworthy: There is no organization in the world today which is more worthy of trust than the church. We all must keep it that way. Trust helps the church run its affairs professionally. Can any one trust you for anything?

3. Accountable: The pastor must keep promises. He must take the initiative to be trusted. Affirm and encourage trust. Walk the talk to avoid credibility gaps between what you say and what you do.[4]

4. Truth: The pastor must inspire, teach, encourage, and be a role model for telling the truth by the way he lives and remains consistent. This is good for the church and the community. Never must any gossip originate from the pastor or any member of his family. Lack of truth destroys confidence of the people in the church and its work. It weakens the moral strength of the church.

5. Reliable: When the pastor says something, it must come to pass. This means you must be sure about anything before you make any statement so that you are relied upon. You must be a reliable source of truth and hope.

6. Humble: Be humble all the time. The Lord teaches us to be humble. In humility we have strength, courage, inspiration, decency, rationality, respect, and thoughtfulness.

7. Respect: Respect people as you would wish them to respect you. If ever there is a place where people can learn about what it means for humankind to respect each other it must be in the church of God. Do not look down upon women and children. Respect them the way you would want them to respect you. God will bless you for that.

8. Patient: Being patient means we take time as events unfold without having to put other people or ourselves under pressure. Never have I found in any church all people doing things on time all the time. Some are slow. Others take time to believe. Some never agree with the rest. Others are selfish. But all belong to the same Lord; the pastor must be patient with all. Be patient to all, the apostle Paul says.

9. Gentle: Do not be rough, hasty, and uncaring in making decisions that affect the life of other people. If they sin, rebuke them in love and care. If they disappoint you, be patient, and tell them that you are disappointed and that they are not supposed to take you for a ride or for granted.

10. Care: There can be people in the church who can be very difficult. Take a genuine interest in them as people. A leader must be likeable. Be merciful. Be courteous and include them in your prayers. Challenge yourself to get them to represent in your lifetime. Ask God to bless you in their sight, for them to see how powerful and responsive to prayer

4. Chalke and Relph, *Making a Team Work*, 25.

God can be. Be kind to them. Teach them to be kind to everyone. If there is someone who needs help, be the first to offer help. That is the way to teach the congregation to be kind. Also in speech be kind as well as in thought and action.

11. Love: God loved us all as he gave us his only Son. The essence of giving must be evident in the pastorate. A giving congregation is a loving congregation. God blesses it for such acts of charity and love. Love is less effective if it is only talked about. It is more effective when it is evidenced and manifests in all activities at the church and in the lives of people.

12. Peace: All congregations that enjoy peace have the power of the Holy Spirit operating within them. Suppress or deal with all fighting spirits in the congregation. Peacefulness must start with the pastor even if he is wronged by anyone, he must remain peaceful. Being peaceful is a challenge, which must be won at all costs.

13. Self-discipline: This is the ability to control oneself. Doing things on time and avoiding life and activity that puts the life and reputation of the church into disrepute is a sign of self-discipline.

14. Receptive: Put your ears on the ground and train your conscience to listen attentively to the needs of the people. Take time to listen to the people's conversations in public and in private. You can tell what they need most and what they hate most. Not all you hear will be of benefit to you or the church but you are better off informed than being ignorant. This is good for decision-making purposes. Work with them to effect change in aspects of the church and their prayer life which can be assisted for the good of their spiritual life.

15. Self-control: Have self-control in all circumstances, no-matter how irritating or sensitive or provocative the situation may be. Most powerful leaders attempt to remain in control of their tempers even in difficult circumstances. Take charge of your mental faculties in trying situations. Then you will make a difference.

16. Spiritual maturity: signs of spiritual maturity are: slow to anger, patience, love, ability to forgive one another, giving time and money, as well as service to the Lord without asking for something in return but waiting upon God for a blessing.

17. Sensitive: This is the ability to understand people and their reaction patterns. Putting others first is a gift from God. Christian leaders who do not do this are, most times, selfish because they think of themselves first. A good leader must be sensitive to the needs of the people. If

you are not happy about something, do not pretend that all is fine. You may be missing a point. Understand what people like and dislike and the reasons attached to those personal positions. This will make your work more enjoyable.

18. Wise: All wisdom to run the church comes from the Lord. Those that feel they are clever to an extent that they can run the church on their own fool themselves. Each leader in the church must seek wisdom from God to excel in God's work. Wisdom comes through prayer, fasting, and meditation.

19. Vision: Where there is no vision people will perish. The pastor must have a shared vision for his congregation. When there are changes in appointment the leadership of the church must carry on the vision to its logical conclusion.

20. Courage: The pastor must be a source of courage for the congregation. There are situations in the church which can be frightening to the congregation but the pastor must inspire the people of God to move on as the Lord instructs.

21. Diplomatic: The ability to help people work through emotionally-charged differences of opinion in ways that build consensus and team spirit. Conflict managers never stop assessing differences among the people they seek to assist overcome controversy and lack of tolerance. There is always a way of talking to a bad person or situation. We must ask the Holy Spirit to lead us in a way that does not cause confrontation, despondency, confusion, disruption, but hope and growth.

22. Inspiration: Inspiration is the ability to express vision, high ideals, goals, and hope in ways that move others towards new thinking and actions. Effective leaders go beyond just being clear, their vision is accompanied by enthusiasm, conviction, and sincerity. Each day of our lives, we must listen to what the Holy Spirit is saying to us as administrators of the church of God. The pastor must get inspiration from God himself. The blood of Jesus inspires us never to weary in our journey of faith. He is the light of the world. The Lord helps us to transform society not by our own power but by the grace and strength from the Almighty.

23. Confident: People will not follow a leader who does not have confidence in himself.[5] They are naturally attracted or keen to follow a

5. Maxwell, *21 Indispensable Qualities of a Leader*, 98.

leader who conveys confidence.[6] People must learn from the pastor how to be confident in all situations and circumstances. Loss of confidence often occurs when one is experiencing problems, but it is the Lord who gives us confidence in such times.

24. Effective communication skills: Communication is always positive interaction.[7] Without the ability to communicate a leader cannot effectively cast his vision and call his people to act on that vision.[8]

25. Discontent with the status quo:[9] Never be satisfied by the way things stand in your church or congregation. Aim to improve the status quo. Great leaders are never satisfied with current levels of performance, they constantly strive for higher and higher levels of achievement.[10] They move beyond the status quo themselves, and they ask the same for those around them.[11]

26. Willingness to delegate:[12] There must be adequate willingness to delegate on the part of the leader. This gives people around you some confidence in your leadership. Delegate freely.

27. God-fearing: Throughout the world, leaders who fear God work with a conscience that is sensitive to what God requires out of their administration. God fearing leaders must have wisdom, vision and the power to care, strength to listen, humility to sustain leadership challenges, and a heart to love that comes from God. Those leaders without these qualities cannot sustain the challenges of leading God's people.

28. Transparent: Make things clear, open, contestable, and leave room for improvement, questioning, criticism, and critical evaluation in all church activity and programs.

In addition to the above, a good administrator must be:

slow to suspect but quick to trust
slow to condemn but quick to justify
slow to offend but quick to defend
slow to expose but quick to shield
slow to reprimand but quick to forbear

6. Ibid.
7. Ibid., 99.
8. Ibid.
9. Ibid., 100.
10. Ibid.
11. Ibid.
12. Chalke and Relph, *Making a Team Work*, 113.

slow to belittle but quick to appreciate
slow to demand but quick to give
slow to provoke but quick to help
slow to resent but quick to forgive[13]

All excellent leaders in the world today anchor their administration on four pillars:[14]

a) Relationships with people;

b) Equipping the people around you to know what they are supposed to do;

c) Attitude, which is the make or break ingredient of success; and

d) Leadership, which is defined as influencing the people around you. It is often noted that in a life time each person influences 10,000 people.[15]

A good leader must always ask oneself the following questions:

1. How can I gain the trust of the people I work with?
2. What is my most important relationship?
3. Whom should I equip to achieve desired results?
4. How can I inspire others to excel in their life and work?
5. How can I grow spiritually and professionally as a leader?
6. How does attitude influence my leadership?
7. What impact is my leadership making on the life of the church?
8. How can my leadership touch the lives of others with a lasting impression?
9. How can I motivate others to be what I am or even better?
10. How can I make a positive and lasting impact on the lives of others?
11. How could I have better communicated what I said?
12. Are people in the church appreciating what I am doing?
13. Is what I am doing in the best interest of the church?
14. Would Christ appreciate what I am doing if he were physically present?
15. Is my life a blessing to other people?

13. Turner, *Christian Leadership Handbook*, 17.

14. Maxwell, *21 Indispensable Qualities of a Leader*, 9–11.

15. Ibid.

Prayer: Dear Father, help me to be an effective leader. Give me the qualities of a good leader. Grant me the strength to be a prayerful leader. Save me from being proud of myself. Help my life to be a blessing to other people. Amen.

8

Financial Administration

WHAT IS FINANCIAL ADMINISTRATION?

In Biblical understanding financial administration is the stewardship of God's treasure; that includes money. It is the management of God's wealth, such as natural resources including gold, which comes from the soil, which is his footstool. People are part of God's economy, placed in charge of these treasures. Dominion and custody of these resources have been placed in the hands of humanity as an active part of God's management team, as reflected in Psalms 8:3–6 and Genesis 1 and 2. God's treasure is meant to benefit the sustenance of the cosmos in the interest of God and us, his children. We, then, as humanity have the responsibility to manage the universe as stewards. Stewards, then, become responsible for the equal sharing of all the resources in the scheme of God. No human being, therefore, must have a greedy monopoly of the world's natural resources without a sense of sharing.

The church needs money to run its programs, which include spreading the gospel of Jesus Christ. Money for the church is also needed to sponsor people who have left their homes, families, and properties for the sake of the work of ministry. Money is required in the church today to feed the hungry, clothe the naked, and take care of the underprivileged. The money must be properly administered in the same way all church members would be accountable to their own funds at personal and family level. The core business of the church is to bring people to Christ and to care for those that have accepted Jesus Christ as their Lord and personal Savior. The church helps Christians to do this function perfectly well. The church finds it difficult to sustain this task without financial resources. Just like the people of Jerusalem who had one family who offered a donkey on which the Lord rode as he entered into the city as they sang, "Hosanna, Hosanna, blessed is he who comes in the name of the Holy One." Others donated their pieces of cloth where the donkey walked. They donated what they had for the successful entry of the Lord into the city. Today the people of God must offer the resources they have in order for Christ to enter into their lives, homes, and towns. Such resources include money.

FINANCIAL STEWARDSHIP IN THE CHURCH TODAY

Financial stewardship concerns our responsibility to live wholly for God, managing our resources to give him glory and to benefit humanity.[1] Financial stewardship touches every area of life and involves our commitment to taking care of everything that God has given us to look after in the world today. It involves the proper use and care of our natural resources. It is what we do with our abilities and talents, and the way we manage our time in relation to God's expectations and our own good intentions. It is the management of all God's gifts to humanity. Stewardship begins with God. He gave his only son to the world. He gave the best he could to save humanity. We, too, can give the best we can for the good of humanity and as a way to show our love to God.

In the Old Testament: God owns creation (Ps 24:1–2; 50:10, 12). He provides land for humankind as he did with his people (Deut 25:19). He owns all (Exod 22: 28–30; 23:19; 34:26) He set principles of the stewardship of property (Lev 19:9–10) and crops were left for the poor. Tithes and sacrifices were important (Lev 27:30–32; Num 18:21–32; Deut 14:22–27). Tithing was a major aspect of Old Testament financial stewardship. Three types of tithing were common in the Old Testament: a) celebration tithe of agricultural products (Deut 12:6–7; 14:22–26; b) a charity tithe (Deut 14:28–29; and c) a tithe for the Levites (Num 18:21–24).

In the New Testament: Financial stewardship involves taking care of a master's property including money, household goods, and people (Luke 12:42–48; 16:1–13). Other texts on stewardship include Luke 12:16–21, Matt 21:33–46, and Luke 17:7–10; the unmerciful servant (Matt 18:21–35); workers in the vineyard (Matt 20:1–16); the two sons (Matt 21:28–32); the talents (Matt 25: 14–30). The task of a good steward is to be faithful and accountable to the master by increasing the assets. The pastor is a trustee of God's treasure.

1. Berkley, *Leadership Handbook*, 405.

WHERE IS GOD'S PLACE IN OUR FINANCES?

God must be in the center of our finances. The Bible says it is more blessed to give than to receive (Acts 20:35). Without him all the money in our bank accounts, homes, and pockets will be used by the devil to cause destruction of human life through unending wars, disease such as HIV/AIDS, theft and armed robberies, terrorism, divorce, and many others. Such is today's carnage. A lot of care must be taken in the use of our God-given treasures. Use your money for the glory of God. God must control our finances from the center and not from the periphery. This makes him in charge of all that happens to our money.

It is not the money that must control humankind. If money controls humankind, then people use it to exploit other human beings. For example, some people sponsor bandits that threaten world peace. There are some callous men who sponsor young women to work as prostitutes in brothels. All forms of human trafficking are a result of the work of the devil in the world today. Even prior to this current problem, human beings were being bought and sold on the market like vegetables and tomatoes in the slave trade era. But if God is in the center of our finances, then we have both power and authority to command the devil away from our financial destiny. The reason why any one of us cannot account for what we use our finances for is because we have not given God a priority to be the center of our finances. The money then vanishes into thin air before we even get it on payday. The devil has laid claim on it before we have any authority on it. To overturn this we must commit our finances to God. We must remember that God has given us the stewardship of ninety percent of what we have and we must give him ten percent of what we have, which belongs to him (Matt 22:21, Lev 27:30–34, Luke 12:48).

WHAT IS THE ROLE OF THE PASTOR IN CHURCH FINANCE?

The Bible says the pastor must be paid from the money that comes from the people he takes care of as his parishioners (1 Cor 9:13–14). But then what amount of control on church finance must a pastor have? It must only be professional, consultative, advisory, and guiding. Yes? He is not a pastor for finance. In most denominations he is an ex-officio member of the finance committee. He must let the lay people run the treasury.

When Jesus appointed Judas to the post of treasurer in the first cabinet it does not mean that the Lord could not be in charge of the funds they had. It was trusted to another person outside the Lord himself.

ROLE OF THE PASTOR IN CHURCH FINANCE AND STEWARDSHIP

1. To be a good steward of God's wealth. The pastor must know how church funds are being used. The pastor must not be a stranger to the financial administration of the congregation or church. However, in some denominations, the pastor may not be a treasurer, though he may be a signatory to the church account.
2. To make sure those appointed to take charge of the treasury of the church are men and women of integrity and high morals.
3. To personally see the accounting of the church and have an understanding of how church funds are running the business of the church. He should not wait to receive the treasurer's report on the day of a finance meeting or administrative board or church council.
4. To ensure that the church has met all its financial obligations approved by the leaders of the church through the treasurer. He must check with the treasurer from time to time. It is his task to ask this question, ". . . have we met all our financial connectional obligations to date" in the administration of church funds at the local church.
5. To call the treasurer and the finance committee (in some instances where the church's constitution has this structure) from time to time to brief you on the state of church funds.
6. To make sure all church account books are sent for audit at stipulated periods of time. This must not be left to the finance committee or its chairperson or treasurer. Follow up to make sure that this has been done. If the treasurer is dragging his feet on this, make an appointment to talk to him in a one-to-one discussion.
7. To act immediately if church funds are not clearly accounted for and if questions have arisen on the misuse of such funds.

8. To verify information on accusations of such missing funds and never to accuse the finance personnel of theft of church funds but to take a pastoral approach in solving the crisis.
9. To give pastoral protection to the finance committee when under unfair attack from the church or a clique or financially inactive individuals who are very difficult to work within the church.

PASTORAL SUPPORT

Money is needed in the church to pay the pastor in order for him or her to take care of the spiritual needs of the church such as preaching the word of God and taking care of the sick, orphaned, widowed, and others in need of pastoral care. There are many people in the world today who are scared away from coming to church because they feel their money is not safe. Others say it will all go and feed the pastor or enrich him. Some times we hear such comments such as: the pastor is milking us to nothing. In general, there is no church in the world today that can pay the pastor an amount equal to the amount of work and service he or she does. What pastors get as their salary, especially in Africa, generally is a lot less than what can sustain his or her family. It is almost nothing, especially for some of those who pastor some rural churches. However, some congregations try their level best to provide other benefits. This gesture of goodwill and generous giving is most appreciated by the pastors. All pastors are financially sustained by God's grace. They are like birds of the air that survive even if they do not plough in the fields, but they live. If there is any pastor who is wealthy, it is just by God's grace.

Typically, pastors do more work for less money than people in other careers. I suppose many people are not aware of the function of a pastor in a parish. They think he preaches on Sunday or Saturday, and that's all. The pastor, a good one, preaches, teaches the word of God, administers weddings, buries the dead, visits and prays with members of the church in their homes. He counsels those in distressed conditions. He administers discipline in the church as well as caring for all members and the community in which he serves. He gets involved in training the laity who is elected into positions of leadership. He administers the sacraments as prescribed in the constitution of the denomination, attends every committee meeting as an ex-officio member. He gets actively involved in the planning of all church programs and puts them on paper in the form of a calendar or lectionary. He attends actively to all spiritual revivals in and outside his own parish. He makes sure that he is actively involved in the men, women, and youth programs.

All these pastoral functions are calling upon him to be in attendance twenty-four hours a day. For example, on Sunday he is preaching, Monday he is resting on his day off, Tuesday he is in the office preparing a sermon, Wednesday he is visiting those in the hospital, Thursday he is visiting in the homes of the members, Friday he revisits his sermon that he left on the table on Tuesday, and Saturday he attends committee meetings in the morning and finalizes his sermon in the afternoon. Sunday he is back on the pulpit. Some home or hospital visitations are done twice a day or twice a week depending on the condition of the patient and the location. Money is needed in the church to sponsor pastoral programs such as those above and many others not directly linked to the pastor's office. It should be known that the pastor spiritually takes care of all his members from the day a human being is born to the day the same human being is buried. To the glory of God the pastor takes care of his flock from dawn to dusk. When his child is sick and word comes that another member is ill, he spares time to leave his own to attend to the wider family of God. He walks or drives distances to visit not his relatives, but children of God. When the church financially supports this person properly God will pour his blessings on it and its members and their families by blessing them with more wealth. This has happened and it will continue to happen in the church of God.

SOME REASONS WHY THE CHURCH NEEDS MONEY

1. To support the pastor's welfare in the form of a meaningful "salary" or "stipend," which allows him to live like everyone else who would need to buy food, clothes, send children to school, pay medical expenses, funeral insurance, maintain a car, buy fuel for its use, and take a meaningful holiday while on leave. The pastor needs these facilities. God will give him all these through the members of the church. The Bible says that: "you will be made rich in every way so that you can be generous on every occasion and through us your generosity will result in thanksgiving to God" (2 Cor 8:11).

2. To pay for all bills at the church such as rentals for facilities used if the property does not belong to the church, electricity, water, telephone, and many others.
3. To buy church supplies such as bread and wine for holy Eucharist and the cups and basins for the same use. The pastor needs a stove in the parsonage, as well as a refrigerator, so that visitors to the parsonage will feel at home. These are replaced when they wear out.
4. To purchase or rent church property, such as the parsonage, where the pastor and his family must stay, or a car that the pastor must use to visit people in their homes when they most need his counseling.
5. To sponsor all evangelistic programs, such as crusades and revivals, that will result in bringing people to Christ. Musical instruments that give our voices perfect audibility and effective communication must be bought.
6. To buy Christian literature that helps our Sunday school programs to grow in our understanding of the word of God.
7. To help the poor in the community by feeding and clothing them as need arises. Money is also needed to run health care programs such as HIV/AIDS prevention and care programs. Care and counseling programs must be accompanied by meaningful and practical financial assistance. For example, assistance must be given to a patient whose drugs must be purchased when they are required.

FINANCIAL CHALLENGES

But the church in Zimbabwe faces critical and unique challenges of poverty, political instability, HIV/AIDS, and brain drain. Most of these originated from financial challenges faced by families and individuals. These problems affect pastoral work in a unique way, but financial challenges help you to see the mighty hand of God especially when you eventually walk through the situation. The words of David in Psalm 23 are a source of strength. So, each pastor faces a unique type of administration of the church. It is then noted that in whatever unique and challenging situation a pastor finds himself the Holy Spirit takes care of such life threatening situations. No matter how unique or frightening your situation in the Lord's vineyard is, the Holy Spirit will take charge and be in control in all seasons. God has a unique way of getting us to solve our problems in a unique way. He opens up avenues that allow us to go around critical problems of life. By the way, what did the disciples say when they were riding in the boat which was about to sink in turbulent seas? They called on the Lord to help them. Jesus said to the stormy sea, "peace, be still," and it calmed. It is not the storms of poverty or HIV/AIDS, money shortage, inadequate food or health care, or shortage of clean water that we must be threatened by but whether or not we are aware that Christ is very close to us, perhaps we are even riding with him in our thoughts, pain, confusion, intolerance, uncertainty, bitterness, anguish, and disbelief. Christ is in the same spiritual flight with us, all we need for peace to prevail in our mind, soul, and life is to call on him with a voice that shows him that we are not only uncomfortable with our situation but that we are in danger. He will respond to such a call with unfailing authority. When your situation is unique Christ will apply unique methods of dealing with it. When it is new he will apply new methods of showing his power over it. When your problem is dangerous God will use dangerous methods of dealing with the crisis. Consider the life of the great leader Moses. When he faced a double edged sword, where on one side the Egyptian soldiers were approaching the people he was leading, and on the other he was facing the Red Sea, God gave him the confidence to face both and trust that he would not be left alone. God used a dangerous method to deal with both fronts and sources of fear, danger, and confusion by destroying the enemy from his back. Both the sea and the soldiers succumbed to the authority and power of God, the God we pray to today.

You may be serving an appointment which you do not like, or running a church whose financial base is uncertain to an extent that it is not clear if the next salary will come. You may be facing an illness which you know will eventually take life sooner or later, and this affects your soul and powers of meditation every day. You may be running a church where the congregation feels strongly that it's time you bid them farewell because you have taken too long with them or they feel you have overstayed. We all do not feel the same and our situations are unique and sometimes frightening. Administer your life in the trust of God. For the church it is God who will take care. Some problems are like fire, your hands are human so you cannot handle the fire and don't want to risk being burnt. But God can handle the fire for you. Remember when he wanted to sent the Prophet Isaiah for a mission. He sent his angels with fireproof hands that never got burnt by the burning coal they had in their hands. When your situation is dangerous God will use dangerous methods to deal with it. His method is always effective. If God wants a program to be realized, it comes out as planned even if there is no money. God will use nothingness to bring about something out of nothing to show his power, just the way he ordered the universe into being out of nothing. It is his choice to use humanity or not to bring about something into existence. God allows shortages to manifest themselves in our life to show us that he has the authority to sustain us out of nothing, or out of a situation of scarcity. We need money to move the church forward; if it is not within our reach, God sustains us in unique ways.

MATERIALISM AND CLERGY

It appears to be a great concern for the church to see a loss of focus for clergy when there is more emphasis on raising funds for the material wealth of the pastor than providing for the poor such as orphans in the church community. At the same time this is not to say that the pastor must be starved in order to focus on raising funds for the poor. There must be a meaningful balance between these two important services for the church. The pastor is entitled to his or her salary and allowances, which must come to him naturally from the church. If it delays, there is always amicable communication to raise the attention on such delay. Some fight for it. Others make a lot of noise to draw attention to such matters. The professional way of doing it is to communicate through relevant channels. There must be a reasonable balance of attention between professionalism and materialism. Excessive love of money remains a challenge for some pastors. The pastor must give training for the laity on how to handle such challenges before they develop into huge stressful situations. There is also the need to be sensitive when making financial demands from the congregation as the pastor may be viewed as too materialistic in his work. A lot of care must be managed. Breathing space must be give to the congregation to plan and provide for him or her. Know your congregation and its financial challenges so that your financial claims do not override the incomes they receive at any given time. The pastor's sermons must never settle such challenges; instead, the pastor should have dialogue with the relevant committees. If the sermon is used to attempt to settle it, the pulpit will witness such convulsions as that of a hungry man who becomes an angry man. Do not claim more than what you have spent if you use your own funds to get things moving in the church. The Lord will bless you in another more abundant way. Doing this would be greedy. But would it be necessary? The Bible says greed brings trouble (Prov 15:27). The pastorate is called of God. Use professional language to say things that may have resulted from an oversight. The love of money must be managed with a lot of care. If you cannot do without money, then this is a challenge to pray about. We have guidance from the Lord when we are told "do not make money the most important part of your life" (Matt 6:19). It is good advice to be reminded that we must seek the kingdom of God first and all other things will be given to us in due course. It works to operate this way. The opposite of this pattern causes problems for most pastors and administrators in the church.

I have heard of some pastors or pastors' spouses who go mad if they do not get their salaries on time. They claim what belongs to them because "I have worked for it," they say. But the way such a claim can be made makes a difference. The best way would be to remind the chairperson of the committee that deals with pastor parish relations. That person will talk to the relevant finance committee chairperson who will, in turn, refer the matter to the treasurer. This can happen in less than one hour, and a salary that had been forgotten can be effected within reasonable time. This method appears to be too long for someone whose salary may be long overdue but it is the most effective way of dealing with the matter in the sense that the pastor will maintain an acceptable rapport with the finance personnel and the entire congregation at large. The laity may be unused to pastors who become jittery about their salaries and allowances. A good approach makes a lot of sense, rather than emotionally demanding what one is owed.

DOLLAR POWER: IS THE PASTOR A SLAVE TO THE LAITY OR THE LAITY A SLAVE TO THE PASTOR?

The answer to this question is "no." Both the pastor and the lay people are of service to the Lord. One of the commonest ways to control a human being is through the use of money. Relatively, big nations control small states through economic power. Donors determine what needs to be done with their money. They call these "designated funds." Money is often used to exploit human beings in many parts of the world today. For this reason it is thinkable that the love of money may be said to spoil some good relations. The Bible says "stay away from the love of money, be satisfied with what you have, for God has said I will never fail you, I will never forsake you" (Heb 13:5). The Apostle Paul tells us that Christians should not be lovers of money, especially if one is a leader he must not be one who loves money (1 Tim 3:3). Instead, we should look to God for security and not money (1 Tim 6:17–19). In this very important aspect of ministry the pastor must be exemplary for all other leaders to follow. But this does not create room for the laity to exploit the pastor. But this is not to say that there is something wrong with money; it's our attitude towards it that needs proper orientation. Money can provide many things, among them social and emotional comfort, conveniences, leisure, education. But it cannot buy health, happiness, satisfaction, joy or heaven. One great difference between the people of God and those of the world in relation to money and material things is their attitudes.[2] God's people use them (money and material things); the world worships them.[3] Lot looked upon the fertile plains of Jordan instead of deferring to Abraham; Jacob schemed to defraud Esau of his birthright; Ananias' and Saphiras' lives ended tragically as they cherished their gold; and Judas committed suicide for a paltry thirty pieces of silver.[4] Both clergy and laity may need to adopt a positive attitude towards money and material things in order to put both to the service of God.

There are many congregations in the world today that instruct their pastor what to say, when to say it, and in whose favor. If he does not do so they have administrative muscle to have him transferred even if he prefers to remain on post for personal or professional reasons. Where such problems occur the pastorate must indeed remain professionally focused in his work. The laity who controls the pastor to the detriment of his work causes, among other problems, a lot of stress to the pastor and the congregation because instead of focusing on his pastoral work he focuses on how to make people happy (instead of how to make God happy about his work). These are survival skills the pastor may apply—against his will—in order to remain acceptable to the congregation that may be fed up with him. But for both the laity and the pastor in this

2. Lunn, *Treasures in Heaven*, 72.

3. Ibid.

4. Ibid.

situation the critical thing is to pray about it and to seek advice from the Holy Spirit. Also, confide in some God-fearing, honest, faithful, and reliable members of the congregation who may be able to provide effective advice. Pray that the Holy Spirit causes you to remain yourself, the one called to serve that church at that time. Be courageous, "for I am with you always up to the end of the world," the Lord says to his disciples. In your unique situation as a pastor and church administrator call for his counsel and his answer will be in your favor.

It is not the intention of the laity to control clergy through money by influencing decisions that are critical to a congregation, but it may just happen. Wealthy people influence major decisions in most organizations, it appears. The church is not exceptional. But the pastor must work and relate to the laity in such a way that they will respect him to the extent that they will not be tempted to let their possessions influence the affairs of the church. Rather, they will be influenced by the grace of God to make the church achieve its spiritual goals with a sense of maturity and responsibility. People with lots of money within the church must be a blessing to others and more so to the church.

It is known the world over that the church cannot be run by pastors alone. Both clergy and laity have an equal opportunity and responsibility to run the church in the most efficient way. None must be a slave to the other, neither must be a boss to the other, and yet both must be slaves of the Lord Jesus Christ.

WHAT DOES THE BIBLE SAY ABOUT MONEY AND GIVING?

i) Sharing

The Bible says that Christians must share what they have with those in need (Acts 2:42–45). In this text, the concept of sharing is the key to the work of ministry. Those who give money to the church for the mission of the Lord Jesus will always be blessed. The church in Macedonia gave beyond expectation and their ability; and entirely on their own they urgently pleaded with the apostle Paul for the privilege of sharing in the service and giving to the saints (2 Cor 8:4). In addition, the members of the church gave themselves first to the Lord and then gave generously to the apostles.

ii) Giving

Giving is the highest level of living.[5] When we decide to give to the Lord or to his servants we must give whole-heartedly. The Bible says, "Remember this: Whoever sows sparingly will also reap sparingly, and whoever sows generously will also reap generously" (2 Cor 9:6). Further, "Each man should give what he has decided in his heart to give, not reluctantly or under compulsion, for God loves a cheerful giver" (2 Cor 9:7). It is wonderful that ". . . God is able to make all grace abound to you, so that in all things at all times, having all that you need, you will abound, in every good work" (2 Cor 9:8). Also, "You will be made rich in every way so that you can be generous on every occasion . . ." (2 Cor 9:11). Again, when the Lord visits us into our inner house, respond from the heart by giving as much as we can. John Wesley says, "Work as hard as you can, earn as much as you can, and give to the Lord as much as you can".

METHODS OF GIVING

There are two main methods of giving, namely "required" and "freewill" giving:[6]

a) Required giving: This type of giving is compulsory; all citizens are required by state law to pay taxes to the government as given in the constitution (Matt 17:24; 22:15–22; 23:23; Luke 18:12; Heb 7:4; Rom 13:1–2, 6–7).

b) Freewill giving: This type of giving is freewill and spiritual; Christians give generously to the church to support its ministry objectives and mission programs. This type of giving is an investment in God (Luke 6:38; Matt 6:19–21, 24; 2 Cor 9:6–7; Matt 19:21). It is sacrificial giving (Mark 12:41–44; Heb 13:16; Phil 4:18–19). It is not a matter of what you have (Luke 16:10; 2 Cor 8:1–2, 5, 7). It is a response to God (Acts 2: 43–47; 4.32–37; 11:27–30). It demonstrates love (2 Cor 9:7; 2 Cor 8:8). It gives us blessings (Phil 4:10; 2 Cor 9b:8–11; Acts 20:35). It has to be planned (1 Cor 16:1–2). It must be personally determined (Luke 19:1–8; 2 Cor 8:9). Giving to the Lord is obedience to God (Gen 22:16–18).

5. Maxwell, *21 Indispensable Qualities of a Leader* 58.

6. For further details on required and freewill giving, see MacArthur, *God's Plan for Giving*, 84–87.

METHODS OF FREEWILL GIVING

i) Tithing

The minimum form of giving or supporting the church is tithing. Tithing is the payment of one tenth of one's income for the financial support of the church and its programs. It is sometimes called proportionate giving. You give according to what you earn or have. There is only one reason why every Christian should be a tither: because it is biblical.[7] It was an Old Testament law. It was a system given by God to Moses for the support of the Levites, the priests. Abraham was probably the first person to give a tithe to Melchizedek (Gen 14:20).[8] He gave out of his own heart and will. He was not forced by the Law of Moses because the law came four hundred years later. He gave gratefully, cheerfully, and systematically.[9] Today's Christians have accepted it as a proportional way of supporting the church. Tithing is a basic principle of prosperity and one of the most important types of giving. When you tithe the Lord blesses you most abundantly. The Bible tells us, "Bring all the tithes into the storehouse so that there will be food enough in my Temple" (Mal 3:10); "And we will bring tithe of our crops to the Levites, for it is the Levites who collect the tithes in all the towns where we work" (Neh 10:37); ". . . and all that you shall give me, I shall give you a tenth" (Gen 28:22); "He who does not work shall not eat . . . Yet we hear that some of you are living in laziness, refusing to work, and wasting your time gossiping" (2 Thess 3:7–13); "The laborer is worth his wages" (1 Tim 5:18). We can give a tithe of the tithe (Num 18:25, Neh 10:38). Tithe is for the Lord's prosperity.[10] Therefore, we must not procrastinate.[11] It must come first before all our bills are paid.[12] This is what it means to seek the kingdom of God first (Matt 6:33). We must tithe on our gross income and the tithe belongs to God.[13]

7. Kendall, *Tithing*, 29.
8. Ibid., 44.
9. Ibid., 45.
10. Chiza, *Blessing Connector*, 63.
11. Ibid., 50.
12. Ibid.
13. Ibid., 63.

a) Why must we tithe? [14]

1. The Bible teaches it (Matt 3:7–12).
2. Christ commands it (Luke 6:38).
3. It is a way of showing love to God (1 Cor 13:4).
4. It is more blessed to give than to receive (Acts 20:35).
5. Our hearts are where our treasures are (Matt 6:19).
6. It is a way of seeding (2 Cor 9:6–13).
7. Christ sacrificed his life for us (2 Cor 8:9).
8. All that we possess comes from God (Deut 8:17–18).
9. It is a principle of prosperity God instituted (Lev 27:30).
10. It connects us to God thereby unlocking His blessings (Prov 19:17, 2 Cor 8:1–5, 1 Tim 6:17–19).
11. We learn from Abraham, the father of faith, who gave a tenth of his goods to the Lord (Gen 14:20, Heb 7:2).
12. "We will store the produce in the storerooms of the temple of our God. We will bring the best of our flour and other grain offerings, the best of our fruit, and the best of our new wine and olive oil. And we promise to bring to the Levites a tenth of everything our land produces, for it is the Levites who collect the tithes in all our rural towns" (Neh 10:37).
13. ". . . I give you a tenth of my income" (Luke 18:12).
14. "Bring all the tithes into the storehouse so there will be enough food in my temple. If you do, says the Lord Almighty, I will open the windows of heaven for you. I will pour out a blessing so great you won't have enough room to take it in! Try it! Let me prove it to you" (Mal 3:10).
15. "God will bless the work of your hands" (Deut 28:12).

b) How must we tithe?

We must tithe a) based on our gross or on our net if we are self-employed, b) first, before all other bills; c) on a weekly or monthly basis, paying it on the first Sunday after each payday; d) cheerfully; and e) truthfully.

14. Ibid., 70.

ii) Sunday offering

This is another form of giving in the church. It involves giving money or clothes or fruits or anything that we consider to be a way of thanking, praising, worshipping, recognizing, and acknowledging the importance of God in our lives as human beings. We give our valuables, including money, to the church as a way of worshipping God in a special way. In the Old Testament times these gifts would be used by the priests to give to the poor, orphans, widows, and others in need, as the religious community would determine. Some of the food would take care of the welfare of the priests. To this day the money that comes in on Sunday during worship service goes towards sustaining the work of the church which includes looking after the poor, orphans, and widows. It also pays the pastors and teachers of the word. The most important principle of giving today "is the more you give the more the Lord will bless you."

iii) Harvest Thanksgiving

This is another form of giving which is Biblical and very effective when understood well by the members of the church. It involves a committed and sacrificial form of giving where individuals in every congregation sets aside an entire month's proceeds such as money or fruits and devotes it to the house of God as "harvest." The phrase harvest thanksgiving derives from Biblical times when the people of God would bring their first fruits or crops to the priests and God's house to bless them and offer them to God. Most people celebrate harvest thanksgiving in the month of July as it seems to coincide with the harvesting of crops from the fields. Those who have modernized this event bring money or other items such as cars or donate houses to the church as a way of thanking God for what he has done in their lives. Others surrender their lives to Christ on this special day of harvest thanksgiving, all to the glory of God. Harvest thanksgiving is a way of worship. The measure you give comes back to you multiplied many times.

iv) Pledge

This is an additional form of giving. An individual pledges to pay all the telephone bills, or electricity bills, or pay the pastor's salary for an entire year or half year or for a month depending on how much the Lord has blessed that individual. This form of giving is also known as commitment giving. Thus, you make a commitment to give as the Lord blesses you in life. It works better when individuals respond to the Holy Spirit which tells them what to give to the house of God. It opens up God's blessings on those who give wholeheartedly.

All forms of giving must come from inside one's heart rather than being forced. God does bring blessings to those who give cheerfully and with all their hearts. When you give wholeheartedly, the Lord will bless you in the present or future generation lineages without fail. God meets his promises as he did for Abraham and Sarah by providing a child to them in old age (Gen 18:1–15) or what he did for Hezekiah by adding fifteen more years to his life (Isa 38: 1–6) or to the widow whose husband left a debt to her and her two sons (2 Kings 4:1–7).

v) Love Offering

Other forms of giving such as love offerings (or blessings to the pastor) are practiced in some churches as the Spirit of God reveals or directs. People bless their pastor as the Lord blesses them. Giving to the Lord is limitless. And, God's blessings to his people are limitless. He gave us his only son to be a ransom for many. He gave us the best, so we must in turn give him the best in our lives.

Prayer: Dear God, please help me to be a good steward of your flock. Save me from the excessive love of money. Give me the blessing to give you the best I can. Thank you for your son Jesus Christ who died for me. Teach my spirit the right way to worship through the giving of my tithe. Your name be praised forever. Amen.

9

Poverty Alleviation in the Church

WHAT IS SPIRITUAL POVERTY?

Spiritual poverty means not recognizing the existence and importance of God as one who gives life, sustains it, and takes care of it now and at the end one's physical life. People in the world may own all the wealth they need but if they have lost their soul, then they have no life. The Bible says only fools say in their hearts that there is no God (Ps 14:1). It is wise to know that God takes no pleasure in fools (Eccl 5:4). When God created humankind he breathed into his nostrils and then there was the first person realized as a human being. From dust came humankind and to dust in death will his spirit return. So when people who were created in God's image say they do not believe in his existence or in his influence in their lives then they are really spiritually poor. Such poverty can only be alleviated through God's power.

SOCIAL AND ECONOMIC POVERTY

Poverty is not a gift from God, it is in effect a curse from the devil; therefore, it should be rejected with the same force as anyone would reject sin. Poor people must fight the devil and send him packing and leave humanity. This is how a poor man remains in the original image of God, who is not a poor man. A church mouse has a very difficult life. It feeds on the remains of food left by parishioners who come to church every worship day. They too are poor. But every person who comes to church is not poor. Not even as poor as a church mouse. A person who comes to church to worship God is not poor, in the sense that he has all the brains to call on God to make him rich—the sense to call on God is in itself a lot of mental wealth. The sense to hear and feel God calling on all people to communicate with him is a lot of wealth for any individual. The gift of having the ability to talk to God is in itself significant wealth, which some people do not possess. God is very wealthy. He created the world without any of us assisting him. He used his own resources to create the world and all its wealth: natural minerals, gold, diamonds, copper, silver—the soil from which it comes is his foot stool. The people who are called by his name and have accepted him as father are his children and have the authority to share in his inheritance of all the natural property that belongs to him. For that reason the church of God can never fit into the description "poor as a church mouse." Reject poverty with a permanent attitude. That is a mature way of dealing with the devil in modern times. All wealth comes from God to us as part of his creation. All forms of poverty must be rejected.

SIGNS OF SPIRITUAL AND ECONOMIC POVERTY IN THE CHURCH

1. Selfishness: Some people feel that they do not want to share resources. The pastor must help the church create a sense of wanting to share what they have, for the good of the entire family of God. This was the spirit of the first church in the Acts of the Apostles (Acts 2:43–47)

2. Animosity and conflict: Some people feel uncomfortable about other people. Animosity is an advanced form of hatred for some. This creates conflict for the church. It also stifles the growth of the church. The pastor must not be part of it so that he is well positioned to help the church out of it.

3. Hostility to other people: Naturally, there are some people in any congregation who feel they hate the leaders of the church or its subordinates. They may not say it in public, but their behavior definitely shows it beyond any doubt. Their statements say it for them. Their comments in public or private meetings confirm it. Given a fair chance to destroy the life of the leaders without being known they would do it. Such hostility must never be allowed in the church or in the community.

4. Jealousy: For some reason there are people in the world and in the church who feel they want all good things for themselves and not anyone else. They feel bad about the success of other people. This is a practice that destroys the church. All congregations must watch out for this evil.

5. Lying: Lying is a bad thing for any person anywhere in the world. Pastors, leaders, and members of the church must never lie even if their lives are under threat. It is a good thing to be known for telling the truth rather than being known for untruth. Both small and big lies destroy the church of God. Make it a habit to tell the truth all the time. Every one will respect you for that and, in addition, it will make life easy for you.

6. Outbursts: An outburst is emotional or uncontrolled behavior or speech in public. It is a very bad practice, especially by a public leader. Avoid it at all costs because it affects your selection of words. When you say an emotionally provoked vulgar word it is very hard to unsay it, especially in public. Outbursts are signs of a serious lack of self-control. An outburst also shows that you have completely failed to sustain an argument. The situation will have taken over your inner capacity to reason things out. The golden rule is "if you are an emotional person, avoid saying much" lest you lose respect forever. Avoid being known for your wild emotions.

7. Creating divisions: People who create divisions in the church do it to their own glory. This is done mostly by people who had problems in their upbringing. They want to be accommodated by everyone including those who were absent when they grew up as babies. They seek attention, which they were denied when they were growing up. But at this stage they are not quite aware whose attention they want to draw close to them. They seek this attention by any possible means. St. Paul had problems with such people in the Corinthian church. All churches must be aware of such tendencies in such people.

8. Envy: Envy is a feeling that you wish you were like another person in terms of success, favor, good will, wealth, and personhood. It is bad practice. It is evil. The church whose members feel this way may do so unknowingly. It is one way the devil uses to control the children of God. It is only fought through prayer and fasting.

9. Feeling hurt by the success of other people: This draws the church to poverty. Never be hurt by the success of other people. Instead pray for their success. That way God will bless you abundantly. If you have the weakness of feeling bad about the success of other people, talk to God about it He will redeem you. Challenge this feeling and be born again.

10. Inadequate knowledge of God: This causes poverty in the church. The pastor must create learning space for the congregation to study the Bible and argue their faith to the glory of God.

11. Spiritual insecurity in the church: When the congregation feels insecure spiritually it behaves in a funny way. Members may fight against each other in public or church meetings. They fight about small things. They gossip. They miss worship services. They stray. They never study the bible. They appear to know everything. They resist purposeful and well-timed positive change.

12. Financial insecurity in the church: People who give less in the church complain most about church finances not being used properly. Congregations must teach their members the blessing of tithing and giving money to the church as the only way to getting wealthier. We all know that the more we give to God the wider God opens the windows through which he will shower his blessings onus. When we get these blessings the church will never become poor.

13. Rabble rousers in the church: There are many people in the church today who are sources of conflict in any setting. They pick statements of leaders or other members, which are well intentioned, and twist them to suit their grievances. They raise questions that the church never expects. They are gossip spinners. They solve personal grievances through unreasonable questions and communications in public meetings. Their language in public meetings is psychologically violent and unpolished. They do this to create tension in the meeting or church.

14. Despising other people: A church that looks down upon other people ends up in poverty. Never despise the poor. All members of the church must be treated with dignity and respect. In the sight of God all people are the same. It is the pastor's role to see that there are no members who despise others and to correct the image of the church in a reasonable way.

15. Grudge giving: The Bible says to be a cheerful giver so the Lord can bless you abundantly. Never give money, or anything, grudgingly to the church because God may not approve of it. It is more blessed to give than to receive. Grudge giving causes poverty in the church and must be avoided.

16. Inability to forgive: The ability to forgive is a gift of God. We must seek God to give us this gift. No one can pretend to have this gift. Jesus had this gift as he demonstrated it at the cross when he said, "Father forgive them for they know not what they are doing." Failing to forgive causes poverty in one's life and in the church. The Lord's Prayer carries this request in a passionate way.

17. A feeling of self-sufficiency: As children of God we learn from God from time to time. No one is self-sufficient in the church. We belong to each other in all circumstances of faith and spiritual well-being. There is no one who knows all. We all depend on God for survival.

GENERAL METHODS OF POVERTY ALLEVIATION

The *first step* to get rid of poverty in the family and in the church is to first acknowledge it. The *second step* is to trace its roots and cut them off. It is not easy to cut one's traditional and cultural roots of poverty. But it is possible to cut ties with the devil that oppresses humanity in social and economic poverty. Wipe out poverty from a position where it will never visit you again. Where then is this position? There are two positions that can defeat poverty as a creation of the devil in every situation and environment.

First position: be prayerful or full of prayer in whatever posture you take when praying. Powerful prayer sends the devil fleeing fast and forever!

Second position: be a consistent cheerful giver. Consistent poverty flees from consistent cheerful giving. This form of consistent giving is called tithing. This is the only way of poverty alleviation in the church today. All other forms of giving are additional to tithing. Any person who tithes in the church today will never be poor in life. The position is a prayerful post. There is no position other than tithing from which a Christian can fight poverty in personal life and the life of the church. Tithing is the only simple, truthful, honest, humble, proportionate, and consistent way of communicating with God at the highest spiritual level ever! The devil has no other equipment to counter Christian faith and conviction to fight poverty when a tither stands firm in this Biblical principle of poverty alleviation.

METHODS OF INVITING WEALTH INTO THE CHURCH AND IN PERSONAL LIFE

When a Christian gets involved in tithing he becomes rich in his life in terms of material wealth, speech, thought, and deed. The following are some methods of inviting wealth into our lives and the life of the church where we are members:

1. We must honor God by our gifts (Exod 35:22). When you give, God remembers you at your critical times in life, such as illness—as what happened to King Hezekiah (Isa 38:1–8).

2. We must give generously to honor God (Ezek 2:68–69).

3. We must give to others, even those from whom we do not expect a return; God will reward us for this gesture of generosity (Mark 9:41).

4. We must give our best to support Christian workers (Acts 28:10).

5. We must give our very best to the church because God is pleased with our gifts (Heb 13:16).

6. We must give our very best because giving reflects God's love (1 John 3:17). God gave us the best of his own life. We, in turn, must give him our very best. Abraham, the father of faith, gave his best. By faith we can give the best of our own. When we give the best of our ability it helps the church to help our people in need (Acts 2:44–45).

7. Wealthy people should give generously (1 Tim 6:17–19) so that God will bless them more abundantly in their business life.

8. Tithing: giving ten percent of all our earnings consistently.

9. Create seminars for the congregation to teach the members of the church who may be interested how to start their own business enterprises. Invite successful business people to address such critical issues such as:

   a) How to start a successful business
   b) How do you sustain a business
   c) The best method of wealth creation
   d) Money marketing
   e) Investment
   f) Purchase of shares in various companies
   g) Property development

These methods of inviting wealth apply in all unique situations of the globe provided we are prayerfully sincere in our moral and Christian conduct. All successful people around the globe have applied these methods and found them working in their personal lives and the lives of their churches. This type of conduct has made a lasting impact on people's lives for many generations. Apply them if you want to be rich spiritually and materially.

STEWARDSHIP OF THE SOUL REMOVES POVERTY

Stewardship of the soul is a very important aspect of our life today. What does it help for us to gain the whole world and lose our soul? We may have a lot of money and property, but to still lose our souls, it will all be nothingness. Our bodies will rot and perhaps become food for worms. But no worm can touch our soul if we are good stewards of it now. To remove poverty of the soul we need to try the following:

1. Read the Bible from time to time and learn from it.
2. Be in meditation (private and quiet prayer) everyday of our lives.
3. Attend church every Sunday, or worship service, and learn something from it.
4. Attend spiritual revivals once every month to grow spiritually.
5. Find and read Christian literature. Frequently learn and apply what you read.
6. Attend Sunday school regularly and learn from the discussions.
7. Engage and participate in Bible study, and its discussion, at a small group level to grow spiritually.

Prayer: Eternal God, save me from the sin of poverty. Give me the power to work as hard as I can and to give to the church for your sake, as much as I possibly can. Bless the work of my hands. Teach me to love the poor. Please give the poor a meal to survive, shelter to call home, something to warm their bodies, and a life worth living. Amen.

10

Stress Management[1]

WHAT IS THE MEANING OF STRESS?

STRESS IS A STATE of unhappiness, boredom, uneasiness, spiritual restlessness, mental pain, and anxiety. It is the non-specific response of the body to any demand made upon it.[2] The way a person responds to it is very important. We have to learn the techniques of how to deal with the stressors to avoid harmful effects of such situations.[3] Stress is the physical, emotional, and mental strain resulting from the mismatch between an individual and his or her environment. It results from a three-way relationship between demands on a person, that person's feelings about those demands, and their ability to cope with the demands.

Further stress is a state that occurs when people: a) are faced with events they perceive as endangering their physical or psychological well-being and b) are unsure of their ability to deal with these events.[4] All administrators of various organizations such as churches, government or other civil society face this problem at one time or another in their lives. Stress is not always easily avoidable. Sometimes it is created by other people. In other instances we create it ourselves. The most important thing to know is how to manage it. Some forms of stress kill their victims. Other forms eat you to death. Other forms just make you sick.

1. For further details on stress management, see Chivaura, "Stress." See also Atkinson et al., *Introduction to Psychology*.

2 Brown, *Surviving the Loss of a Loved One*, 95.

3. Ibid.

4. Atkinson, *Introduction to Psychology*, 555.

COMMON EMOTIONAL RESPONSES TO STRESS

a) Anxiety: The primary response to a threatening situation is anxiety, which means the unpleasant emotion characterized by worry, apprehension, tension, and fear.

b) Anger and aggression: Anger is a common response to stress. It sometimes results from stress that develops from one's failure to receive an expected reward or achievement or goal. When the effort to reach a goal is blocked the drive to have it in vain motivates behavior that will lead to the desire to injure the object or person causing such frustration. Anger in this capacity develops into aggression. Students at one of our mission schools went on strike because they wanted meat in their relish (though it is nationally in short supply). They broke classroom doors and smashed windows at their dormitories and classrooms. Mature adults express their aggression verbally rather than physically, only in extreme cases do they exchange blows. But it is notable that direct aggression toward the source of frustration is not always possible or wise because sometimes the source of frustration is vague or intangible. In such a case the anger is directed to any soft target on which to vent out such anger. This often happens when the source of frustration is so powerful that an attack would be dangerous.

c) Apathy: Apathy is withdrawal. Children who feel powerless to challenge their unapproachable parents can just withdraw. Or they will engage in passive resistance. This withdrawal can eventually develop into depression. All administrators must be sensitive in their work so that people will not withdraw because the leader is "untouchable." Be simple, approachable, loving, firm, and caring!

COMMON SIGNS AND SYMPTOMS OF STRESS

When a leader is stressed there are signs that show themselves. If you are not happy about something, watch out for these signs:

1. Poor productivity or poor performance at work
2. Poor time-keeping
3. Blaming other people for one's own mistakes
4. Sleeping during meetings
5. Loss of sleep
6. Lack of concentration
7. Fatigue

8. Poor eating habits (e.g., answering the phone while eating or chewing)
9. Difficulty in comprehending new procedures and policies
10. Lack of cooperation
11. Lack of interest in anything
12. Withdrawal
13. High incidences of error in one's work

HOW CAN I KNOW IF I AM UNDER STRESS?

a) Emotional signs:
   1. Blaming others for your mistakes
   2. Easily irritable
   3. Being hostile
   4. Decline in self-esteem
   5. Being suspicious
   6. Paranoia
   7. Withdrawal
   8. Depression
   9. Frustration

b) Behavioral signs:
   1. Decreased productivity
   2. Forgetfulness
   3. Preoccupation
   4. Humorlessness
   5. Anti-social behavior (e.g., theft, prostitution, bribery)
   6. Suicides
   7. Accidents

c) Physical signs:
   1. Muscle tension
   2. Headaches
   3. Overeating
   4. Undereating
   5. Heavy drinking
   6. Upset stomach
   7. Restlessness
   8. Difficulty in sleeping
   9. Cold hands and feet

10. Sweaty palms
11. High blood pressure
12. Elevated pulse

d) Illnesses that may result from stress:

1. Hypertension
2. Heart disease
3. Cancer
4. Lung ailments
5. Cirrhosis of the liver

HOW CAN STRESS BE REDUCED?

i) Health wise:

1. Pay attention to your diet by reducing fatty foods, sweet things like cakes, sweets.
2. Avoid alcohol.
3. Take regular aerobic exercises: walking, jogging, cycling, and swimming.
4. Avoid smoking.
5. Get regular and restful sleep.

ii) Work wise:

1. Manage your time effectively.
2. Delegate some of the responsibilities to other people.
3. Keep all your work at the office as much as possible to avoid conflict with family responsibility.

iii) Family wise:

1. Accept who you are and live within your means.
2. Avoid borrowing without the possibility of paying back.
3. Share with friends and family members issues that seem to be stressful to you.

FUNDAMENTAL CAUSES OF STRESS

Stress is essential to life but it can be a cause of death. It is essential because it is part of what God has created in human beings to show that he has the power, which he has extended to us as his children, to control us and the rest of creation. The following are some of the causes of stress in most work situations in Zimbabwe and perhaps the world over:

1. Poor relationships with colleagues or spouse or both
2. Lack of job security
3. Changing work demands
4. Fear of failure
5. Stringent expectations at work or in life and family (e.g., grilling by the boss, or a heated argument with spouse, or a difficult deadline)
6. Stringent deadlines
7. Isolation, especially in highly confidential roles
8. Poor work/home interface
9. Change of appointment
10. Marital insecurity
11. Marital instability
12. Unstable family conditions

The following Life Events Scale was developed by Holmes and Rahe in 1967.[5] They called it the "Social Readjustment Rating Scale." It measured life changes of persons. These are some of the major causes of stress. Effective counseling must address these problems.

Life Event	% Value
Death of spouse	100
Divorce	73
Marital separation	65
Jail term	63
Death of close family member	63
Personal injury or illness	53
Marriage	50
Fired from job	47
Marital reconciliation	45
Retirement	45
Health change of family member	44
Pregnancy	40
Sex difficulties	39
Gain new family member	39

5. Atkinson, *Introduction to Psychology*, 567.

Business readjustment	39
Death of close friend	37
Son or daughter leaving home	29
Trouble with in–laws	29
Wife begins or stops work	26

MOST COMMON EFFECTS OF STRESS

1. Increase in making mistakes
2. Increase in clients' complaints
3. Increase in supervisor's complaints
4. Poor timekeeping
5. Close all communication channels with others
6. Relationship problems at home and at work
7. Alcohol and drug abuse

HOW CAN YOU MANAGE STRESS?

The Stress Management Society has identified 10 tips to manage stress as follows:

1. Avoid nicotine, alcohol, and caffeine. Keep yourself hydrated by drinking water.
2. Exercise regularly to produce a good mood in the brain.
3. Relax by telling yourself "I have a choice in every situation."
4. Get enough sleep.
5. Take a rest if you are ill.
6. Agree with people or keep quiet for awhile. Avoid an entire life of fighting.
7. Learn to accept what you cannot change. This will help you avoid bitterness.
8. Listen to your body. When tired, hungry, thirsty act accordingly.
9. Learn to say "no" when appropriate without feeling guilt.
10. Manage your time.

TECHNICAL METHODS OF MANAGING STRESS

1. Discuss problems and challenges with colleagues.
2. Share tensions and frustrations with colleagues.

3. Consult medical or counseling service providers without delay if you feel stressed by something.
4. Accept that you have a problem and that you need assistance to reduce or alleviate the problem.

NATURAL METHODS OF MANAGING STRESS

Jogging, basketball, bicycling, football, swimming, karate, canoeing, squash, tennis, walking, horse-riding, bowling, skipping, golfing, handball, table tennis, and running.[6]

WHAT DOES THE BIBLE SAY ABOUT STRESS?

1. Delegating work can alleviate stress (Exod 18: 13–26).
2. God is our refuge in times of stress (Ps 62: 1–8).
4. Wait upon the Lord (Isa 40: 30–31).
5. Understand that God is always with us (Rom 8:31–39), (Matt. 2 8 : 18–20).
6. Understand that everything works well for the good of those who love God (Rom 8:28).
7. God cares about our stress (2 Cor 4: 8–12).
8. Do not let stress cause you to worry (Phil 4: 4–9).
9. Call on God; he is always there for us (2 Chr 7:14).

THE PROBLEM OF BURNOUT AND ITS MANAGEMENT

In general, burnout emerges from continuous stress. Burnout describes the syndrome of emotional exhaustion, depersonalization, low productivity, and feelings of low achievement. It occurs in most work situations. It does not respect anyone's age, educational qualification, social status, gender or religious orientation. It catches, often by surprise, anyone who invites it.

Burnout comes when we think or act as if we alone can do the work of ministry that God is calling our team to do.[7] To avoid burnout, effective training for all pastors must be a continuous process. Refresher courses are a very helpful vent or window of hope for pastors and other leaders put in charge of large groups of people. Delegation of responsi-

6. Brown, *Surviving the Loss of a Loved One*, 96.
7. Logan and Short, *Mobilizing for Compassion*, 168.

bility is another strategy to avoid burnout for pastors and other leaders. A good example of a Biblical leader who faced burnout was Moses (Exod 18:17–18). Jethro advised Moses of an effective way of administering a huge congregation by training some junior officers to deal with some issues while he handled the major ones. This was delegation of responsibility.[8]

MOST COMMON SIGNS AND SYMPTOMS OF BURNOUT

1. Severe exhaustion
2. Frustration
3. Aggressive attitude and behavior
4. Hostile attitude and behavior
5. Feeling of hopelessness
6. Forgetfulness
7. Lack of interest in one's work and life
8. No feeling of excitement in life
9. Coming in late
10. Being absent continuously
11. Taking nothing seriously in life

METHODS OF MANAGING BURNOUT

1. Take time off duty to replenish. Take it upon yourself to refresh your mind through rest and getting out of stressful situations by going out with friends and colleagues. Be away from business for awhile to breathe new air.
2. Talk to colleagues about your lack of interest in anything. They will advise you to take life as a safe journey and that the hurdles you face are a way of testing and strengthening your power to survive critical stages of life such as depression or mental breakdown.
3. Seek professional counseling. Do not suffer alone. Share your concerns, stress, emotional feelings, and pain with somebody you trust whose confidence you can rely on.
4. Find out the possible source of burnout and restrategize. Do not wait for situations to deteriorate, act fast to avoid being crashed to depression by forces external to your life. Believe in yourself and

8. Ibid.

that what you do in life is pleasing to God in whose power the devil trembles.

5. Go out of the environment and mix with others at various gatherings such as church, golf club, soccer, or any game of your noble choice.
6. Pray about it instead of ignoring it. Believe that through prayer you have overcome it. Nothing is impossible before God Almighty.
7. Alternate routine activity. Avoid doing the same thing all the time. This creates monotony.
8. Actively participate in workshops if they are organized for you. Do not shun meetings with other professionals who are there for your benefit. Ask questions and generate a lot of discussion in such workshops. This will help you gain confidence in yourself.
9. Ask other talented people to take up certain tasks.

THE PROBLEM OF DEPRESSION[9]

Depression, just like burnout, comes out of severe and continuous stress. This is an emotional state of being deeply sad, stressed, helpless, and discouraged. It usually happens when a person encounters serious continuous problems without any solution in sight.

GENERAL CAUSES OF DEPRESSION

1. Seeing life as a succession of burdens, obstacles, and defeats
2. Negative self-perception, e.g., feeling self deceived, inadequate, worthless, and underperforming
3. Attitude of self-blame in every aspect of life
4. Self-pity in critical aspects of life
5. Negative view of the future, e.g., seeing continuous hardship, frustration, and hopelessness. Seeing only the dark side of life and overlooking the positive leads out of depression
6. Loss of people through death or divorce or prolonged separation remains some of the most powerful depression-producing events of life

9. For more detailed discussion on depression as a subject of counseling, see Collins, *Christian Counseling*, 119.

7. Feeling sinful and guilty
8. Family conflict
9. Anger
10. Loss of close relatives or associates
11. Negative thoughts

CHARACTERISTICS OF DEPRESSION

1. Low self-esteem
2. Feelings of worthlessness
3. Lack of hope
4. Feelings of negative thoughts about oneself
5. Self-criticism
6. Pessimism
7. Thoughts of self-destruction such as suicide
8. Social withdrawal
9. Neglect of normal duties
10. Feeling of apathy
11. Loss of energy
12. Fatigue
13. Neglect of personal hygiene
14. Loss of appetite
15. Lack of interest in normal activities such as work, sex, religion, hobbies, and education
16. Numerous complaints about aches and pains
17. Loss of sleep
18. Poor eating habits

EFFECTIVE COUNSELING FOR DEPRESSION

1. Develop social support networks
2. Effective intervention including open discussion about the problem
3. Behavior change guidance
4. Influence change in thinking or perception of critical issues
5. One-to-one discussion with other persons feeling depressed
6. Create an atmosphere of hope for such persons who may be depressed

HOW CAN DEPRESSION BE PREVENTED?

1. Trust in God
2. Understand the nature of the depression
3. Find support networks
4. Reach out to others
5. Keep physically fit by getting involved with exercise

SKILLS FOR DEALING WITH DEPRESSION

1. Learn to handle anger through self-control.
2. Control self-defeating thoughts.
3. Manage your stress well by coping with demands with a positive mind.
4. Stimulate physical fitness through jogging or any form of exercise.

Prayer: All merciful Father, please help me walk through all situations with trust in you. Touch and control my life. I am weak, you are strong, and I depend on you for wisdom, vision, inspiration, and guidance. Save my soul from the challenges and problems that cause burnout and depression. Inspire my thoughts and motivate my thinking. Help me to depend on you for everything. Amen.

11

Pastoral Care and Counseling

WHAT IS PASTORAL CARE AND COUNSELING?

COUNSELING IS PART OF pastoral care. You cannot counsel someone unless you care for that person. It is often noted that "people don't care how much you know, until they know how much you care."[1] Good pastors throughout the world are those who care most for their flock. Pastoral work is all about caring for the Lord's people. Counseling is all about change.[2] It is about people who want to change, people who don't know how to change, people who need help to change, people who resist change, those who seem unable to leave their current circumstances and accept the help of others to change.[3] Counselors work with people who are overwhelmed by circumstances or changes in their lives, people who have no idea how to cope or what they can do to bring about change.[4]

Pastoral counseling as an aspect of care is the process whereby clients or persons seeking spiritual, social, emotional, or psychological assistance come to the pastor and discuss their concerns with him in confidence. Some of the persons who come to the pastor for counseling expect the pastor to give them answers to their questions and solutions to their problems. Others do not expect the pastor to give answers and solutions but just want to share with the pastor. The latter are just looking for a shoulder to cry on. They just want to empty their burdens or problems. They need a safety valve. Pastoral care involves being available for someone needing spiritual attention and care. Pastoral counseling

1. Maxwell, *21 Indispensable Qualities of a Leader*, 103.
2. Collins, *Christian Counseling*, 3.
3. Ibid.
4. Ibid.

needs divine authority,[5] which is derived from Christ. Christians must counsel (Col 3:16, Rom 15:14). Some clients who approach the pastor in need of counseling will be highly immobilized by evil, suffering, and meaninglessness or other overwhelming causes.[6] Pastoral counseling is a process that helps an individual to release any form of tension or stress or frustration within himself by sharing it with the pastor in confidence. Pastoral counseling is, therefore, a process of intervention whereby the pastor intervenes in the search for answers and solutions to a given problem. The pastor must never own the problem because it already has an owner. His pastoral responsibility is to help the client seek, search, and find a solution to his own problem. If the solution that is found works well, the client will be proud to know that he has the potential to solve his own problems. If the found solution fails, the client cannot blame the pastor for such a failure, but he will appreciate the pastor's effort and attention given to the problem. So the pastor's function in pastoral counseling is to care for the client and to empower him to engage in a discourse leading to a solution of his own problem.

Pastoral counseling involves taking time to pay attention to someone who has approached you with some form of a problem. The critical thing in pastoral counseling is listening attentively. Show concern. Be sympathetic to the client. Most importantly, be empathetic. This means taking the client's problem as if it were your own. This places it in a better perspective and in a position to be helpful.

QUALITIES OF A GOOD COUNSELOR

1. Respect your client.
2. Sincere, truthful, and honest.
3. Supportive to your client.
4. Competence. Discuss issues with an open mind without being shy.
5. Confidentiality. Keep confidential information to yourself unless permitted to refer it to another person.
6. Ability to empathize. Understand the client as if you were inside his or her situation.

5 Adams, *Christian Counselor's Manual*, 15.

6. Collins, *Counseling and the Search for Meaning*, 40.

7. Ability to refer. Know your limitations, personal battles, and emotional problems that may fail you in your effort to assist the client. This helps you to refer some of your clients to another professional.

SKILLS REQUIRED FOR EFFECTIVE COUNSELING

1. Respectful: respect the client to earn his or her confidence.
2. Genuine: make real commitment to be involved in the situation of the client.
3. Confidential: keep all information to yourself.
4. Attentive: listen carefully so you can help the client.
5. Empathy: put yourself in the situation of the client without being swallowed.
6. Clarity: make sure you understand the issues involved.
7. Reflective commenting: make positive and encouraging comments during discussion.

TYPES OF PASTORAL COUNSELING

The following types of pastoral counseling are important for the pastor and many others involved in counseling: crisis, referral, educative, confrontational, group, and depth counseling.[7]

1. Crisis counseling (2 Cor 1:4) involves the pastor getting involved at the turning point of an individual towards or away from greater personality wholeness. If the pastor has to be an effective minister he has to get involved at the time when someone is in pain and stress, assisting that person to cope with the pain he will be going through.

2. Referral counseling is a means of using a team effort to help a troubled person. It employs the division-of-labor principle as the basis of inter-professional cooperation to assist an individual who needs help. The pastor recognizes that he does not have, cannot have, and does not need to have expert knowledge in some areas that is required for an individual, if all possible help is to be given. At the same time, he realizes that there is an important task for

7. Clinebell, *Basic Types of Pastoral Counseling*, 160.

him to be done in the situation. Referral ministry is not a sign of weakness on the part of the pastor.

3. Educative counseling (Mark 1:22) is a counseling process whereby the pastor helps the individual in pain or stressful situation to foster personal growth within his own situation. The pastor provides a platform that helps the individual to understand, evaluate, and then apply the information that is relevant to constructive coping with particular life situations. This type of pastoral counseling provides the establishment of rapport and disciplined listening which involves the self-discovery of facts, concepts, values, beliefs, skills, guidance, advice, wise decision making, and handling of hard situations.
4. Group counseling is a natural form of counseling by a pastor who is essentially a group worker and addresses personal challenges that are faced by several individuals at the same time. The pastor uses privileged information to assist individual persons in the form of a group. The pastor takes great care never to mention names of individuals being assisted in that process. He must not imply certain known situations of individuals or groups.
5. Depth counseling is a long-term helping process aimed at affecting depth changes in the life of an individual in a stressful situation. This type of pastoral counseling helps the counselee to uncover and deal with hidden feelings, intra-psychic conflicts, and repressed early life memories. It is a complex, time consuming process and the pastor may sometimes have to refer the counselee to a competent psychotherapist. This type of counseling has the following aims:
    a) Raises individual's self- awareness by listening to his feelings and experiences carefully
    b) Helps individual's insight awareness by providing in-depth understanding of one's own feelings and relationships
    c) Permits the individual to discover self worth
    d) Goes deeper within oneself in terms of emotions
    e) Self-directedness, autonomy, and the setting of goals
    f) Self-acceptance, which leads to the acceptance of others
    g) Discovery of self-joy, being oneself.

6. Confrontational counseling (Ps 85:10) involves speaking the truth in order to help an individual. This type of counseling calls for the pastor to confront the individual with realities of his situation and help him discover his responsibilities in it. This helps the individual towards repentance or confession and then forgiveness. It provides an opportunity for reconciliation between an individual and the self. This opens up new frontiers of knowledge.

OTHER FORMS OF COUNSELING

a. Bereavement counseling:

This has to do with providing pastoral care to a person who has lost a loved one. What makes this type of counseling complicated is that no matter what you say as a way of comforting the client he will never get back the lost life. So the only best thing to do at that stage of the loss is to identify with the client's pain. That is being empathetic. It helps the client feel that a shared problem is half solved. Here are critical tips in counseling the bereaved:

1. Be the first person to arrive at the home of the person who is experiencing the loss.
2. Ask the client if there is any help you can offer.
3. Follow them in their funeral arrangements and assist them when you feel they are stranded as a family.
4. Do not shed tears, for this will increase the client's pain.
5. If the client is losing their physical grip or control you can help him maintain a balance as your conscience tells you.
6. Do not make comments like "God has done his will," because it is not God's will to cause pain and suffering to his people.
7. Remember that your presence is a sermon on its own even if you don't say a thing. God will speak to your client on your behalf.
8. Do not over laugh if a joke is said. Remember any move you make or word you utter is subject to any interpretation. Keep your image at the pastoral level.

9. At the end of the funeral talk to your client, giving words of comfort before leaving the premises.
10. Re-visit the client after a day or two to assess how he is fairing. This is the most problematic time as loneliness and many unanswered questions will be a source of trouble.

b. Marriage counseling:

Some people say there is no perfect marriage in the world today. Neither has it ever existed. This means each marriage has its shortcomings. Here are some of the challenges faced by most marriages: Unfaithfulness, unplanned pregnancy, coming home late after work, unexplained telephone calls or text messages, dishonesty in financial affairs, unplanned spending, bad breath, releasing gas while asleep, bad odor, quarrelling and fighting, lack of respect for one another, poor relations with in-laws, old age, retirement, wanting too many children, loss or lack of sexual interest, coping with menopause, difficult children.

The role of the pastor in these marital challenges is to minister to clients in order for them to see every marriage as God's invention. Every marriage is unique. If it falls into a problem, it requires unique sets of solutions. The pastor must seek God's guidance.

METHODS OF MARRIAGE COUNSELING

a) Individual counseling: Individual counseling involves the one-on-one counseling of a client by the pastor. Dialogue must produce desired results within a given period of time. Take quality time with each member that you feel needs your counseling and ask God for the best approach that will not offend the individual. Explore the crisis with caution and utmost care. Remember, you can never be an effective counselor unless your client has developed some confidence and trust in you. You must also help your client build the confidence and trust that is good enough to enable you to assist that individual.

A very good pastor must be able to identify both the joy and problem areas of individual members of his congregation. Each situation is unique. Some individual families approach the pastor with a marital problem. Others are shy or fear the pastor, fearing the lack of confidentiality. Whichever way this information gets to the pastor he must find a helpful approach to assist the needy situation. It takes great effort on the part of the pastor to approach the client without being invited. You will have to make a choice between letting your client rot in their problem or helping them out, in spite of the way you got the news that they are not happy at home.

b) Group counseling: Group counseling involves addressing critical and common social, moral or emotional problems facing several members of the congregation at the same or different times in their lives. Thus, the pastor gives them care all at once in a single address or group discussion. Names of individuals or known problems are handled with care in one sermon or discussion or teaching lesson. Some of the problems facing individual members or groups within one congregation may include separating or divorcing couples, collapsing businesses, corruption, criminal behavior, and general indecency in society of church.

The issues raised above on the list of marital problems are just the tip of an iceberg. There are a lot more problems not listed, which are critical for many families. The role of the pastor is to see to it that the family of God, entrusted into his hands, is relatively happy. This is critical because happy families make a happy congregation and church.

When the pastor discovers that several families in the congregation face the issues raised in the list above he can organize marriage seminars or marital discussion groups or marriage conferences that will deal with these problem areas.

This group counseling may also deal with single parenting challenges which may not be grouped together with married people. Various groups must be convened depending on the issues at stake in their life and social orientation.

In each of the counseling cases the pastor must never be judgmental in dealing with his clients. Offer advice, guidance, care, and prayers not with bias but with love.

METHODS OF HIV/AIDS COUNSELING

When you counsel for HIV/AIDS you are dealing with: grief, mourning, sorrow, sadness, depression, gloom, rejection, misery,[8] stigma, and stress. Know that you are dealing with loss management. So handle it with utmost care. Your word selection must be sensitive to comforting the client and encouraging the spouse, children, relatives, friends, or in-laws to look beyond the current crisis. Do not make comments that

8. Mhlanga, *Christian Aids Task Force Manual*. 7 (10).

add more injury to pain like "Aids kills" or "all of you must be faithful to avoid death" or "have one partner ladies and gentlemen." These comments may not be suitable for this occasion.

HIV/AIDS counseling has become one of the most challenging problems of our time in the church and community today. When a person tells you that he or she is HIV positive do the following:

1. Appreciate that person for coming and opening up to that extent, or for breaking up the silence.
2. Identify and empathize with his or her problem.
3. Pay as much attention as possible to what that person needs from you.
4. Check at what stage their status is so that you can refer him to the appropriate professional.
5. Find out if he or she belongs to any care and support group. If not, advise him or her to join one for peer support.
6. Share information with them on access to other caregivers and anti-retroviral treatment or any other forms of assistance.
7. Create a sense of confidence in that person and assurance that God cares for all human beings as they are created in his own image.
8. Afford the client a lot of discussion space to empty all fears, frustrations, stress, questions, crises, and causes of loss of sleep.
9. Pray about all the issues raised during discussion and then give assurance to the client to understand that the church is a healing community (1 Cor 12:24–27).
10. Give as much hope and encouragement as the Lord allows you to reveal to the client.
11. Provide confidence in the client by telling him that the church is a sanctuary: a safe place for sharing, telling, and listening.[9] It is a safe space for caring, healing, and construction of confidence. It is a place of spiritual and physical connections between individuals and God. Also, as pastor teach your congregation to understand this function and be involved in interpreting the role of the church in fighting stigmatization.

9. Facing AIDS. *Challenge, the Churches' Response*. 79.

12. Help the client to get rid of self-hate by giving the virus in him a biological meaning and not a moral meaning that sees humanity as sinful or rebelling against God. And let the client understand that wickedness and evil do exist in the world and we are all bearers of both goodness and wickedness—that is what we all have in common.[10]
13. Direct the client to helpful Biblical texts that provide hope, courage, and inspiration: nothing can separate us from the love of God (Rom 8:38–39); in our weakness we are sustained by his Spirit who lives within us (Rom 8:11, 26; Eph 3:16); God is with us even in the midst of sickness and suffering, working for healing and salvation even in the valley of the shadow of death (Ps 23:4); God is love (1 John 4:16, Eph 3:16); love helps you to look past offenses (1 Pet 4:8); we must be known for our love (2 John 1:5); God is redeemer (Eph 1:7); God is preserver (Matt 6:25–33).
14. Help the client to overcome self-denial, shame, fear, isolation, and a sense of hopelessness by talking about his needs, challenges, and problems openly.

ROLE OF THE CHURCH IN HIV/AIDS COUNSELING

The pastor must help the congregation to be of service and assistance to HIV positive persons, and those that care for them, by giving them hope, encouragement, and healing. The major role of the church to the HIV infected and affected is to show love. Love is the most precious gift the church can ever give because it is the only universal language and the only universal stage of civilization the world has ever known.[11]

1. Teach the congregation to have a positive attitude towards them.
2. Create a community of trust and care.
3. Fight stigmatization within the church community.
4. Inspire the congregation to give them company so that they are not lonely: "we do not live to ourselves and we do not die to ourselves. If we live we live to the Lord, and if we die we die to the Lord; so then, whether we live or whether we die, we are the Lord's." (Rom 14:7–8).

10. One Body Vol. 2. *AIDS*, 12.
11. Dube, ed., *Africa Praying*, 117.

5. Encourage the congregation not to be judgmental in attitude (John 8:2–11). Jesus says, "Neither do I condemn you . . ."
6. Organize group retreats with the support groups and facilitate discussions. Involve them in the planning.
7. Teach the congregation to understand that sexuality is a gift from God (Gen 1:27–28) and that it requires responsibility, forgiveness, and respect.
8. Remind the congregation about Jesus's attitude towards social outcasts: he healed a crippled man even on a Sabbath, (Mark 3:1–6); he had time to talk to a prostitute at the well of Jacob (John 4:1–28); he touched lepers (Matt 8:3, Mark 1:41, Luke 5:12–13); he took the hands of the sick (Mark 1:31; Matt 9:25); he touched blind eyes (Matt 20:34, John. 9:6, Matt 9:29); and he touched deaf ears (Mark 7:33, Luke 22:51).
9. Guide the congregation to provide spiritual and physical healing (John 9), (Luke 13:10–17). The church is born out of Jesus so it must touch the untouchable.

HIV/AIDS SUPPORT GROUPS

A support group is the coming together of individuals for support in dealing with a shared concern or experience. They meet to support each other in facing challenges related to their medical conditions. The pastor must encourage the creation of support groups within the congregation. This is vital because the church must be in front in the fight against this problem.

Aims and advantages of support groups:

1. To remove isolation of individuals affected and infected
2. To provide personal, emotional, and spiritual encouragement
3. To create a safe space for interaction and freedom of speech
4. To provide social and economic support
5. To promote self-help support
6. To improve quality of life
7. To fight and remove stigmatization and discrimination
8. To share feelings and experiences

9. To promote self-confidence
10. To empower individuals to be open about their status
11. To share resources, ideas, and information

WHO NEEDS SUPPORT GROUPS?

a. The infected
b. The affected
c. Health care givers
d. Facilitators of support groups

Prayer: Merciful Father, you care for me everyday. Help me to care for others everyday. Teach me to love those who may be thought of as unlovable. Teach me to see your presence in other people even if they may not be as fortunate as I might be. Let my words be a source of comfort to those who hear them. I kindly ask that you help my life to be a blessing to other people, especially to those in difficult circumstances. Amen.

12

Motivation

WHAT IS MOTIVATION?

PASTORAL MOTIVATION IN THE church refers to those aspects of ministry that motivate the pastor and the congregation to feel the need to serve God. It is that powerful and irresistible spiritual desire or longing to serve God in various ways. What makes motivation pastoral in this understanding is the theocentric (God centered) aspect of the concept. It is different from motivation in general which is just a desire to do something. That which serves as reason for the pastor and the congregation to love God is pastoral motivation. Although pastoral ministry is a calling to serve the Lord as a motivation, the professional aspect of it also serves as a social motivation. The professional aspect has to do with other benefits such as the pleasure to serve humankind through the provision of pastoral care and counseling, moral guidance, leadership, and educational training to the community.

Motivation can be described as the reason or passion or rationale for someone to do something. It can be spiritual or emotional. Spiritual motivation is an in-depth feeling for the need for closeness to the Lord, and a sense of wanting to work for and belong to him, to which one cannot fully explain to an outsider. It is a sense of unconditional longing to serve Christ and the church that has no reservation. It is a feeling of longing to be with the Lord in eternity. Results from motivation include acts of worship, faith, and even charity at the highest level.

The most important reason why people come to church is their love of God and what they benefit from the Christian values taught by the church. Additional reasons include their desire for fellowship with other Christians and the personal emotional security the church provides them. The church is a source of comfort when a member is in the midst of personal or family problems.

Spiritual motivation is, therefore, a form of getting church members to love God with all their wealth, soul, mind, and spirit for the good of their own life and that of the church.

In general, motivation is based upon need, which may be real, created or imaginary.[1] Because of these needs, each person produces an assortment (different sorts or forms) of reactions that are called drive.[2] Need is, then, the key to all our behavior and it motivates us. A hungry person is driven to eat by the need for food. If there is no need, then we do not get to do things. To motivate is to incite to action.[3] Motivation is, therefore, an incentive get someone to do something. The basic human motivation for a Christian is salvation. We must motivate each other as Christians to look forward to this great achievement. It is something we can help each other work on. Thus, accepting Christ as one's personal Savior derives from the need to receive salvation from God himself. It is an intervening variable, which is used to account for factors within the organism, which activates, maintains, and channels behavior toward a goal.[4] For example, churches or congregations that take care of their pastors fairly well motivate the clergy to work hard in their appointments. In commerce and industry businesses that look after their employees well can be assured of profitable results. If the human resource base is fairly well remunerated, the company's performance is likely to do better than if the conditions of service, including salaries, are not favorable. Motivation is, therefore, concerned with factors that give behavior direction and energize it.[5] A cheering congregation motivates its preacher to do even better in his presentation. A tithing church motivates its members to achieve greater financial projects that bring people to Christ, such as outreach programs or mission work or educational programs for the needy.

1. Turner, *Christian Leadership Handbook*, 83.
2. Ibid.
3. Chaplin, *Dictionary of Psychology*, 325.
4. Ibid., 325–326.
5. Atkinson, *Introduction to Psychology*, 361.

FACTORS IN HUMAN MOTIVATION

The following factors in human motivation may need to be understood to help us as leaders to motivate people to achieve their goals.[6] Factors for human motivation are need driven. All pastors must have a needs assessment within their congregations because performance is related to needs. For example:

1. Physiological needs: These are the basic bodily functions necessary to survival such as eating, drinking, breathing, and many others. The Bible teaches us that we must work in order to get food. The pastor needs to work to get food and drink. God created us in a way that has allowed us to depend on him for our physiological survival. He breathed life into us as human beings so we can fend for ourselves. The ability to use our brains enables us to work and live for Christ. This must motivate us to work hard.
2. Safety and security needs: These are the basic needs of protection of self, loved ones, and property. The most important safety and security of our lives come from God himself. If we are safe in God's hand, there is nothing that can get us away from such safety. We are, therefore, most secure in Christ than in any other power. Adequate protection comes from God. We are human because God has made us so. We are part of what God is and therefore our needs are God's needs and God's needs are our needs. We can therefore get these if we trust Christ with our lives through whom all things are possible.
3. Achievement needs: This involves the desire to accomplish something. It motivates persons to set goals and work toward them. All Christians aim to live with Christ at the end of this life. This motivates us to remain in Christ while he remains in us. To achieve the goal of having eternal life we must learn to live the way Christ wants us to live.
4. Personal interaction: This is the need to be with other people. It motivates one into social activities and other actions that will bring him into contact with people. God has sent his son Jesus Christ to save our lives. He demonstrated an effective form of interaction

6. Turner, *Christian Leadership Handbook*, 83 ff.

with human kind. Christ took human form in order to help us understand his love and kindness.

5. Recognition needs: These are ego needs where one has the need for recognition, attention, independence, status, power, authority, and prestige.
6. Worth needs: These are the needs to be wanted or considered important or worthy. It is basic for humankind to feel useful.
7. Order needs: These are centered on the desire for neatness, punctuality, and completeness in any assignment. We derive orderliness from God himself. He is the center for our completeness. We learn punctuality from him, for he did all things in the appointed time and he continues to do so. From him we learn the essence of order, neatness, punctuality, and completeness through the way he created the world.
8. Love needs: This is human kind's desire to be loved. If you feel loved, that motivates you to love others or to be a good person worth of love. Love is God's design for humankind to live in harmony. It helps us to be Christlike.

HOW CAN THE PASTOR MOTIVATE A CONGREGATION TO ACHIEVE ITS SET GOALS?

1. Involve them in your planning and setting of goals.
2. Delegate authority and follow-up objectives at appropriate stages.
3. Allow them to make decisions on your behalf and let them be accountable for such decisions.
4. Give proper recognition for accomplishments.
5. Ask them for ideas and opinions. This is a principle of involvement.
6. Place members into small action groups to create team spirit. Make them follow up on each.
7. Find spiritual solutions from the Bible to difficult questions and problems.
8. Equip the laity for challenging, but achievable, tasks.

9. Ask some of them who are talented to lead in the training of their peers.
10. Once or twice in a year take the leaders out for a workshop relating to their work areas.
11. Plan an outing with couples for fellowship to create a lasting relationship.
12. Organize get-togethers in the form of dinners or potlucks with the leaders and invite speakers from outside the congregation to speak on a variety of topics.
13. Create a spirit of sharing in the form of a family potlucks, at the section or location levels.
14. Go out for spiritual and educational tours with the junior church, or youth, or adults of the same age groups.
15. Take special weekends out with the junior church.
16. Group-praise the congregation when they do something great for the church.
17. Identify and praise individuals for their outstanding performance in the work of the church. Give them credit where it is due.
18. Recognize special talent amongst them and give tasks as a way of motivating officers and members of the church.
19. Ask groups of people such as youth, single parents, women's and men's fellowships to sing during worship service.
20. Identify individual talent and make use of it to the glory of God.
21. Know each member by name and a few good things about that person.
22. Be friendly to all members in spite of small or major differences they may have with you or your spouse or relatives or close friends in the congregation.

When all of this happens, the Lord's work is found to be full of joy. This means even if there are problems in the church, just like in any organization, you feel motivated that Christ is with you every step of the way in your ministry.

SMALL THINGS THAT DEMOTIVATE THE CONGREGATION

1. Doing everything by yourself. Give them tasks and responsibilities so they feel like a part of the entire administration of the church.
2. Criticizing without offering meaningful suggestions. This causes despair.
3. Intolerance when they make genuine administrative mistakes such as breach of protocol.
4. Exposing their foolishness in public. Talk to those who may have made mistakes in private and rebuke them decently. Pray with them too.
5. Paying no detailed attention to individual problems.
6. Comparing rich and poor, educated and uneducated, skilled and unskilled, clever and not so clever, young and old, spiritually weak and strong.
7. Despising those that do not talk favorably about you.
8. Despising the morally weak and materially poor.
9. Hating your enemies. Love them as the Bible says.
10. Keeping grudges and finding it hard to forgive.
11. Lack of consistency.
12. Carefree attitude.
13. Lack of meaningful concern when members are in crisis.
14. Identifying with one group in the church at the expense of the rest of the church.
15. Relying on one group or constituency or person in the church for everything including decisions.
16. Too harsh on people over trivial issues that have very little effect on the spiritual life of the church.

THINGS THAT HINDER SELF-MOTIVATION[7] FOR THE PASTOR

1. Poor self-image
2. Depending on external influence
3. Negative attitude to certain people
4. Fear of failure
5. Laziness
6. Postponing tasks
7. Poor self-understanding
8. Lack of self-courage
9. Lack of self-will

Prayer: Heavenly Father, give me the motivation to work hard to please you, not mankind. Motivate my thoughts, deeds, and actions to suit your will. Teach me the best way to motivate your church to achieve meaningful set goals. Guide my pace and steps towards achieving worthy praise for completing tasks that fulfill your heart's desire, not mine. Save me from demotivating your people when they seek to please you. Guard me from being jealous. Forgive my evil thoughts and negative attitude towards other people even when they are more successful than me.

7. Turner, *Christian Leadership Handbook*, 47–48.

13

Public Relations

MANAGEMENT OF PUBLIC RELATIONS IN THE CHURCH

IN 1987 THE BRITISH Institute of Public Relations defined public relations as the planned and sustained effort to establish and maintain good will and mutual understanding between an organization and its publics.[1] In the church social and spiritual relations are public relations. They play a very important role in the life of the church. They must be sustained properly to maintain good will and mutual understanding among believers. In the secular world, for instance, for those in marketing, advertising, or any special area where the public relations exercise is called for, public relations are defined in their own way. But in all situations, a very good public relations practitioner does two things: a) is humble and b) is able to continue learning at all times.[2] Both points mean that a public relations practitioner must have the ability and willingness to find out things related to the organization.[3] In the case of the church the pastor must be willing to learn more about the church and what it stands for, the ability to learn more about the Lord and being his disciple, and making disciples for him. The pastor must also have the ability or capacity to learn more about the church in which he practices his ministry of administration. A pastor who has a poor relationship with his congregation lives in stress most of the time. This affects the

1. Jefkins, *Public Relations*, 7.
2. Ibid., 17.
3. Ibid.

work of the church. The following are necessary qualities that make the pastor a good public relations practitioner:[4]

1. Ability to get on with all kinds of people—this means understanding, tolerating, and not flattering people.
2. Ability to communicate in spoken or written language.
3. Ability to organize—this means planning.
4. Professional integrity in professional and private life.
5. A critical sense of imagination. All sermons in the case of a preacher call for this quality.
6. Ability to find out or research truth or information for the good of the organization.

Everywhere in the world pastoral work is about relations. The only way a pastor can be effective in his work is to create good relations with his parishioners or the community. Never can any person be a good pastor if his relationship with the congregation is strained. If the congregation hates the pastor for some reason, they will not in any way appreciate his work. No matter how dynamic a pastor can be, people will never see the positive side of his work unless his relationship with the church is good. Even if the pastor is very good at preaching, if his relationship with the membership is strained, his sermons will never rise above just an interesting lecture or story about the Bible and its actors. His sermons will just be another drama.

By all means, the pastor must have a lovable personality and a father or mother figure in the congregation who is, in terms of relationship, approachable by all the members of the church. Those that consider themselves rich, poor, educated, unskilled, professional, or people of any description must converge and acknowledge that their pastor is their spiritual leader. Those with sharp differences must be accommodated at the pastoral desk. The pastor must, therefore, create pastoral space for all members of the congregation to interact with each other and with him too. To create good relations with his members the pastor must be friendly, honest, firm, trustworthy, reliable, accountable for all his actions, truthful, faithful, blameless, confidentially oriented, respectful, have a sense of humor, praise worthy, and God fearing.

The most important public relations function of the pastor is to link people to Christ, and vice versa. The pastor must create favorable condi-

4. Ibid., 17–18.

tions so that humankind will choose Christ as their personal Saviour. The pastor must drive, call, direct, guide, convince, convict, deliver, shepherd, witness, and win people for Christ. So when the pastor buries the dead, marries people in church, preaches, teaches and administers sacraments, he is creating a positive relationship between people and God. All these services are pointers to the creation of a lasting relationship between God and humankind.

WHAT DO PEOPLE SAY ABOUT THEIR PASTOR?

When people see a pastor they make assumptions. For example, he must not make a mistake. He must not sin. He must not fail. The same assumptions apply for his spouse. For them a pastor is a man or woman of God. The pastor takes the image of God: loving, patient, truthful, slow to anger, caring, humble, comforting, helpful, non-selective in paying attention, and most importantly being available day and night for anyone who needs pastoral attention. For most people the pastor must be holy. He must not disappoint any one. He must not take sides when there is a dispute. For some people the pastor must never be on leave or take a day off; he must always be there for his flock.

This image is very difficult to maintain although an attempt can always be made. In the light of these expectations, the pastor must just be himself or herself: being human. All that needs to be done is to make adjustments between being human, being male or female, being a father or mother to a family, and at the same time being responsible for a spiritual family: the church. Responsibility and attention between the two are far too vast and demanding that a pastor who is not prayerful will not be capable of managing both families. St. Paul says of elders of the church that they cannot run the church well unless they are able to take care of their own families. Most pastors fall into the trap of paying more attention to one of the two. If you can't manage both, either you pray for strength and wisdom to do both effectively or you just have to quit the ministry or the third option is just to pretend things are fine when they are not. All the three options are operative in the life of many pastors up to retirement or even death. The most important thing is to keep relations afloat between yourself, the family and the church. A meaningful call to the ministry can take care of both very well. Those who fail to maintain both cannot blame either for their failure. In fact, it has been proven beyond reasonable doubt that both can compliment each other most effectively.

IMAGE MANAGEMENT FOR THE PASTOR: CHECK LIST

_____ Is my relationship with God at its best?
_____ Am I leading the church the way God wants?
_____ Is my image a reflection of what God expects?
_____ Is God proud of me?
_____ What areas of my spiritual life need to be improved?
_____ What is my most difficult problem for which I need God's help?
_____ What is my weakness?
_____ What is my special gift?
_____ How can I improve the life of other people?

These questions must help the pastor improve the management of his image both before God and the church or congregation that he pastors. It is an evaluation of the self. Self evaluation is part of image management for the pastor. It should not be taken lightly.

THE PASTOR'S PERCEPTION OF PEOPLE

Most pastors take appointments at places they have never been before in their lives as pastors. There is a tendency for pastors to think that all congregations are the same. It would appear that all chairpersons of finance at any given church are the same: they are hard-hearted or perhaps just strict? Treasurers are worse than finance chairs because they never have the heart to release money even if the church council tells them to do so. They treat church funds as if they are their own personal money. Other pastors feel some laypersons are more powerful than them in terms of decision-making, especially on financial issues. The laity oversteps its authority over the clergy. Some laypersons think the pastor is their employee. So you see, they pay the pastor; they buy him clothes; food; a vehicle, or commonly a bicycle in the case of rural pastors, a house to stay; organize his annual leave; pay him travel and telephone allowances; or give him bus fare, just the way they treat a domestic worker or a groundsman. All parish or circuit pastors who are working under these conditions are working under difficult conditions. They are not free. If you are working with people who control the "way you breathe" or the way you must walk or laugh or read your Bible as a pastor, then you need to teach the congregation a lesson or two on the importance of keeping amicable relations between the pastorate and the congregation.

But the pastor must carry his or her own image reflective of the profession of pastor. People will follow the image that the pastor is portraying of himself or herself. If you show an image of a beggar or of being a poor and hopeless person, then the people will call and understand you as such. If you portray the image of a person who is confused, or someone who lacks self-confidence, then the people you lead will know you for your confusion or for your lack of confidence. So, it is important for the pastor to portray an image that reflects the character of God himself. This is the confidence that pulls the church forward in all circumstances. In the same time respect, you must respect the laity as you would wish them to respect you.

SENSE OF HUMOR

Since humankind is created in the image of God, his sense of humor is a gift from God.[5] This gift must be controlled and well cultivated to an extent that clean wholesome humor will relax tension and relieve a difficult situation more than anything else.[6] It is a great asset in the life of a pastor or anyone in administration. Humor lends pungency, originality, and eloquence to sermons.[7] The most successful preacher is one who possesses a keen sense of humor in combination with God's grace.[8] Like one missionary said, "I have never met leadership without a sense of humor, this ability to stand outside oneself and one's circumstances, to see things in perspective and laugh. It is a great safety valve."[9] You will never lead others far without the joy of the Lord and its concomitant, a sense of humor.[10]

All relations in the church have to do with humor: the ability to be free and be capable of sharing lighter moments of life such as cracking jokes with friends, relatives, and colleagues. Laughing and joking are good ways of releasing tension, stress, frustration, and poor concentration. Every person needs this type of life where you can be freed from boring routines of life.

5. Sanders, *Spiritual Leadership*, 59.
6. Ibid.
7. Ibid.
8. Ibid.
9. Ibid., 60.
10. Ibid.

Anyone who is in administration must make every effort to search for situations that help him access a relaxed atmosphere where you can laugh your lungs out. Over-laugh once a day and that keeps you going in your daily challenges. Over-smile once a day and that makes a difference in the way you look at what appears to be an unworkable situation. Create a sense of humor each time you wake up in for a new day. Or, record your sense of humor each day. This will carry you throughout your week or month or year. Even if you are in a terrible situation, try to look at it positively. Joke about it. You do this not because you are underestimating the challenge but you are challenging the problem so that you may see it through in a unique way. Every problem or challenge has a positive side. Approach all problems from that perspective. Record the humorous aspect of your problem and get that to help you sail through the challenge.

There are people who never laugh for an entire week. They prefer to keep their tension, frustration, and stress to themselves. This eventually eats them to death. Do not be one of these unwise men and women!

TENSION IN CHURCH ADMINISTRATION

Tension is one of the prices an administrator pays if he is to succeed in the Lord's work.[11] It is not possible to avoid it. But continuous tension must be avoided by all means.[12] This means that every situation must not be viewed with an attitude of tension. Tense pastors will produce tense followers. If you are tense, you need to pray, sing, and preach loudly to release the tension. Constant tension prohibits good administration because it is a deterrent to sound administrative judgment in critical matters. If the situation at the church is very tense, defer critical decisions, if possible, because the chances for making costing errors are very high. Tension and rationality are enemies. If you make an administrative error in a period of high tension, both correction and face-saving become extremely painful.

The following are potential sources of tension,[13] which, if possible, you need to avoid or find effective means to deal with:

1. Health problems
2. Fatigue
3. Inadequate qualification for a task or responsibility

11. Turner, *Christian Leadership Handbook*, 209.
12. Ibid.
13. Ibid.

4. Pressure from interest group
5. Self-underestimation
6. Unresolved problems create carryovers, which are not health for any administration
7. Handling too many responsibilities at once compromises strength and energy
8. Lack of trust in colleagues and followers
9. Procrastination (postponing decisions or actions to a later date)

HOW DO YOU GET RID OF TENSION?[14]

1. Admit and appreciate that there is tension.
2. Develop a positive spiritual attitude towards it (Prov 23:7).
3. Understand that some tension will help you grow spiritually.
4. Relax and turn it to Christ. We learn from his passion story and what he went through to save humanity from dying in sin.
5. Pray for wisdom to handle the situation (Jas 1:5).
6. Talk about it with other administrators or leaders.
7. Keep trusting in the Lord even if it appears that prospects for any hope are far-fetched.
8. Get enough rest (Eph 3:2).
9. Teach yourself to be bold. Train your mind to contain and sustain crisis.
10. Develop self-confidence.
11. Regularly exercise in the morning or in the evening.
12. Take yourself out for dinner or for just meeting friends.
13. Develop self-trust that you are on top of the situation and tell it with conviction.
14. Do not share your tension with people who are likely to discourage you or cause more harm than good.Find a good listener and confide in him.

Prayer: Dear God, please set right my relationship with you because I am a sinner. I turn my back on you every day in my thinking and action, but you are always there for me. I seek your presence in my life. Amen.

14. Turner, *Christian Leadership Handbook*, 211.

14

Common Problems in Administration

PRIDE

PRIDE IS SIN OF whose presence its victim is least conscious.[1] It is very possible that you can be very proud without knowing it. Three tests can be used to find out if we have succumbed to the problem of pride:[2] a) test of precedence: how do we feel if another person is selected for something we could also have been chosen? b) test of sincerity: when we praise our rivals do we mean it? c) test of criticism: does criticism arouse hostility or resentment in our hearts and cause us to quickly justify our actions?

The Bible says that pride leads to shame (Prov 11:2). Whoever wants to be proud of himself must take a look at other people and weigh himself against them to see if God's image in him is better than it is in them. If he discovers that he is a better image of God than the other people, then perhaps there is every reason for him to be proud of himself. In the world today, even before the beginning of time, pride was not and has never been God's virtue or characteristic. And yet we are created in his image. How come the image does not reflect the original personality? So, if pride is not God's characteristic and we are created in his image, then pride is our own image and not God's.

When a pastor falls into the problem of pride he does not see other people as important as himself. He does not see the image of God in other people the way he sees it himself. His measurement leading to this conclusion is derived perhaps from social and economic perspective. We should all guard against the temptation of pride. It can destroy the

1. Sanders, *Spiritual Leadership*, 143.

2. Ibid.

church in the sense that some people will be classified as less important than others. Those viewed as less important will in turn fold themselves into emptiness in terms of active participation in the church. Their potential will be less recognized. The church will suffer from their non-participation. Of what good then will this be?

Pride is not good for any leader or individual. When God looks at us all he is satisfied with the way each one looks like him in spiritual stature. Others are ugly while some are handsome or beautiful in our own eyes and standards, but in God's view we all carry a meaningful image. The Bible tells us that pride will be punished at the end of time (Prov 16:5) because it does not carry the interests of God who created humankind in his image. In other instances we are told that pride ends in destruction (Prov 16:18). Who wants to get destroyed for being proud? It's a sin to despise other people because you are full of pride. Notably, pride cuts us off from God and others (Luke 18:9–14). In some instances we may even be worse than those who we think are less important than us.

In his letter to the Romans the apostle Paul says that there is no place whatsoever for proud boasting in the life of Christians (Rom 3:27). In addition, he says to the Corinthian church that God chooses to reveal himself to the humble and not to the proud (1 Cor 1:26–31). At the same time we realize that God opposes the proud (Jas 4:6) because not many people can build their humanhood from a person who is proud of himself. If you feel you are proud of yourself, you need to pray, fast, and ask God to liberate you from such a problem.

JEALOUSY

Jealousy is feeling very hurt about the success of others. It is a notorious sin. It carries all qualifications for hell, just like any other sin. Apart from inviting hell, jealousy is a bad thing. Would you feel good if someone were jealous of you? It is an important aspect of life to pray that one is not jealous of other people. God's message to us is very clear about jealousy. Throughout the Bible we learn that:

1. Jealousy is foolish (Eccl 4:4).
2. Jealousy can destroy someone (Job 5:2).
3. Do not envy those who do wrong (Ps 37:1).
4. Jealousy steals away peace (Prov 14:30).
5. Jealousy is a powerful enemy (Prov 27:4).

6. God doesn't want us to share our devotion (Deut 4:24).
7. Jealousy can cause rash behavior (Acts 7:9).
8. We should not be jealous of other Christians (Gal 5:26).
9. Jealousy has no place in a Christian's life (Titus 3:3–5).

FEAR

Fear is a feeling of withdrawal, inadequacy, emotional emptiness, and being at loss with everything around a person. In administration fear is a terrible enemy. It takes advantage of the weak minded. It prohibits a person from making tough decisions of life. Tough professional decisions call for a tough administrator. In administration fear must never be given a chance because it destroys ambition, desire, focus, vision, hope, meaning, self image, power, authority, integrity, and personal dignity.

The Bible teaches us that if we fear anything, God will protect us (Gen 15:1). It is good news for all of us that God will not forget us (Gen 46:3). Christians do not need to fear anyone (Ps 27:1). God strengthens us (Ps 46:1–3), and we should not fear darkness or violence (Ps 91:5), or bad news (Ps 11:2–7).

When you are not sure of what decision to take as a pastor in a crisis situation pray about it, fast about, and ask for advice from a close colleague and your supervisor.

POPULARITY

This is an instance whereby an individual places all interest on himself. It is an emotional state of being self-centered in all or some aspects of life. It involves drawing all attention to oneself. Popularity is a sense of self-importance.

Whether we like it or not there will always be people in the church who want popularity. They will go a long way, using any possible method, to find it and retain it. They will use any language in their favor to earn it. They will use anyone who succumbs to get it. Learn from the Lord himself. He never had time to search for it. Ask yourself, "Am I being popular with people or with God"?

The Apostle Paul fought it when the Corinthian church was affected by it. He attacked it saying, "When one says I am Paul's man, and another I am for Apollos are you not all too human? After all, what is Apollos? What is Paul? We are simply God's agents in bringing to the faith. Each of us performed the task . . . allotted to him: I planted the seed, and Apollos watered it; but God made it grow . . . We are God's fellow workers" (1 Cor 3: 4–6, 9).

The Lord says of popularity: "Woe unto you when all men speak well of you." One day Bishop Stephen Neil said to theological students: "Popularity is the most dangerous state imaginable, since it leads on so easily to the spiritual pride, which drowns men in perdition. It is a symptom to be watched with anxiety since so often it has been purchased at the too heavy a price of compromise with the world."

Any bishops, superintendents, pastors, and laity in positions of leadership and administration in the church today, who seek popularity and not Christ at any level of the church, make life extremely difficult for the church, as more often than not they are very difficult to work with. Their priorities are keenly at variance with normal ecclesial expectations. Tough luck!

EGOTISM

Egotism is one of the repulsive manifestations of pride.[3] Egotism itself is the practice of thinking and speaking much of oneself, the habit of magnifying one's attainments or importance.[4] It is dangerous in the church because it leads one to consider everything in its relation to himself rather than in relation to God and the welfare of his people.[5] You see, this is a foolish way of doing things! Give glory to God and not to yourself. Is it not embarrassing to be proud of oneself for some kind of achievement when you discover that there are other people who have achieved better tasks but have let other people take respectful notice of it? In the church we say let other people raise your fame, instead of you raising your own, lest it is noted how infamous you are! This is administering the church in a unique way; the least famous becomes the most popular. They earn it, not impose it. It is administratively out of fashion these days to impose an impression on people. A lasting impression is one that a leader earns from the people, not the imposed one. Egotism is a peril of leadership.[6] What type of a leader are you?

3. Ibid., 146.
4. Ibid., 143.
5. Ibid.
6. Ibid., 142.

DIMINISHING RESOURCES

One of the commonest problems in the church in Africa today, just like in any other developing world, is that of diminishing (inadequate) resources. The people who support the church by way of tithing are just two thirds of the membership in most congregations. This makes it difficult for the church to support its budget. The pastor and the entire leadership must, therefore, be very innovative to find other means to support the working programs of the church. In terms of personnel, the church is not spared by migration where the pastorate feels better off elsewhere than in their current appointments. Those who go overseas for further education never return as expected after their courses. The return rate for such pastors who go overseas for studies is perhaps one in every ten. Most find jobs and permanently stay where there are better working conditions.

PROCRASTINATION

Procrastination is the practice or habit of delaying in carrying out one's responsibilities or duties until a later time just because you do not feel like doing it right away. It is a common problem, which most administrators find themselves in. For all church work, time is never plentiful enough to procrastinate on programs and events. All congregations must work with a calendar, which points the leaders to dates, activities, and venues. These must not be procrastinated on or postponed. Rescheduling must be done only in isolated instances. It is the pastor's function to supervise the church to avoid the procrastination of its schedules and programs. The leaders of the church must be trained top operate in this pattern. Some leaders may drag their feet in understanding this pattern of working, but be consistent in enforcing this workmanship.

SPECULATION

Speculation refers to guessing. It is a problem if the pastor leaves everything unexplained so that the congregation is left to guess what is going on in the church. One of the most significant functions of good leadership is communication. No one in the congregation must be left to guess about what is going on at the church. All programs must be put in the open for all to see and participate in. Do not leave everything to the members to speculate. If there is a problem within the congregation, an explanation by the relevant committee or pastor or any other leader must be given. Speculation can destroy the congregation because people will gossip about what they think must, or has been, done. This misleads constructive engagement where church members can otherwise talk openly about what they dislike or feel has gone out of hand without being victimized or sidelined. It invites backbiting, which is not healthy for the church.

NOSTALGIA

In every congregation there are people who feel they were better off with the previous pastor than you as a spiritual leader. Whether we like it or not, one third or half the congregation at any given time move with the momentum or impact of the previous pastor's administration for the first four to six months of your arrival at the new church or congregation. They take time to adjust to you and your pattern of leadership. But then you also must adjust very quickly to avoid leading a new congregation with the organizational methods, and subsequent impact, of your previous parish or congregation or experience. All congregations are different and deserve to be treated just that way. In several instances those congregations that are happy with their pastor feel their relationship should not have been disturbed by a transfer. But a wise pastor must observe this behavior and adjust accordingly. They feel the previous pastor must not have been changed because they enjoyed working well with him. When you make a mistake, they regret your presence among them. They judge your performance on the strength of the previous pastor. They compare your statements, dressing, language, emotions, temperance, sermons, administration, rapport, children's behavior, pastoral care, and professional image. You must prove to them beyond any reasonable doubt that you are there to build on the good things done by your predecessor. You apologize for his mistakes even if he is long gone or has passed away. If you cannot match his standard, demonstrate that you are in his footsteps giving the best to them, though you cannot do it exactly the same way he used to do his work. Let them appreciate the difference between you and the other pastor. If you want to introduce new ways of doing things, it is important to take your time to learn what is going on first before proposing changes. Sometimes if the changes are too quick, they will dismiss or misunderstand them. In other instances they will resist the changes without being open to you. But, of course, some might easily understand the new pastoral dispensation, without any nostalgic tendencies.

DEVIATION

When the pastor asks the lay leadership to do something and they do the opposite instead, that is called deviation. This behavior may be deliberate or not, but it is still deviation. When the congregation asks the pastor to do something for the good of the church and he does the opposite of their request instead, that is deviation. This affects the proper running of the church in one way or the other in the sense that there will be loss of respect for either part, or some form of suspicion on either part. It may also result in lack of trust for the pastor from the congregation or vice versa.

One of the most difficult pastors or church leaders to work with in the church today is one who deviates from what has been agreed by consensus, or the majority of people, in an officially and properly constituted meeting. Such a pastor or leader changes goalposts at random, making life very difficult for peers and colleagues. If you deviate from expectation or agreed principles of doing things, you must explain the reasons for deviation and the extent of the deviation. This means communication is critical in running the church. A pastor or leader who changes goalposts unexpectedly makes life uncomfortable for the church. If you deviate from normal procedure or practice, involve the people affected by the change in the process or planning or organization if possible. Continual deviation in church administration leads to dictatorship, which makes life very difficult for the church. The church of God is led in humility as all pastors and laity are there as servants of the Lord and not masters of the people. Deviant behavior in the church is least expected, especially on the part of leadership. It can destroy the church of God in a very visible way. If destruction is not the final result from such deviation, it may cause cracks in the work of the church in that particular congregation.

CONDESCENSION

Condescension refers to a practice or habit or attitude that tends to show that someone thinks he or she is more intelligent and important than anyone else. It is a problem that is evident in several contexts in many congregations and churches. Some elite, academia, wealthy, and professionally acclaimed persons in business and civil society who find themselves as members of certain congregations have this problem. Some pastors have this problem as well. They feel that the fact that they are called makes them so special that they are above everyone else. They feel everything in the church or congregation must start and end with them or on them. Being a pastor has mostly to do with servant leadership. There is nothing special about being called for the higher office of ministry. There is nothing special about being a leader. It is just a God-given opportunity to lead, or simply show others the way certain things can or must be done at a particular point in time. Given an equal opportunity, others could do it even better. So, for all leaders anywhere in the world, and at whatever level, it is very important to realize the credibility of being humble. In administration we say there is no substitute for humility. It earns respect. It is a virtue and a gift. It has a lasting impact on people's lives for any leadership at all times.

The problem of condescension manifests itself in many forms including, but not limited to, looking down upon others in the same congregation or church, or frowning at decisions that originate from the poor or less educated constituents of the same congregation. The pastor must operate above these perception limitations, instead concentrating on the all-inclusive graces that the church intends to communicate in any denomination worthy of its calling to serve and save humankind. Those people in the church who feel they are wealthy, educated, professionally-oriented, and skilled in various labor fields must view themselves (or be viewed) as a blessing to the church in that the church may then, because of those blessings, not have to hire or pay for services for which they can provide as part of their commitment to serve the Lord. If they view others (or the pastor) as less important than them, then there is an attitude problem which the pastor must professionally be well-equipped (and educated or capacitated) to handle with meaningful confidence and lasting impact. In addition, the pastor must pray about this problem of condescension to receive guidance from the Holy Spirit so he can help those members of the church affected by it consciously or unconsciously.

OPPOSITION

Opposition in the church is as good or as bad as it is in the secular world. It is a price tag for any leader, but the leader must seek to discover the reasons for it.[7] However, the leader must not reject it, or be arrogant about

7. Marshall, *Understanding Leadership*, 91.

it, or be ruled by it, or personalize it;[8] rather he or she should develop a positive attitude about it as it may be a source of spiritual growth.

POSSIBLE REASONS FOR OPPOSITION IN THE CHURCH[9]

i) Resistance to change.
ii) Lack of information.
iii) Fear of uncertainty about the future.
iv) Oversight of important concerns.
v) Careless use of power or authority.
vi) Jealous
vii) Envy.
viii) Careless and unreasoned statements.

Opposition (constructive or destructive) is a good thing for any organization because it gets people in leadership positions to never relax but remain accountable, not only to the people they lead but to God, as well. All that is required for the organization to work well is for it to be managed by a sensitive conscience that seeks to build the church and not destroy it. It also requires to be led and be received by a maturity that does not seek self-interest or selfishness. What matters most is how you respond to it. The ability to handle opposition in the church or any organization by any leader at any level of administration tells a big story about the spiritual maturity of that particular leader. Some leaders fume over small things that have nothing to do with Christ in the case of spiritual leadership. The best way to deal with such personalities is through *prayer* and *constructive engagement* on a one-on-one basis.

CHARACTERISTICS OF MOST OF THE OPPOSITION IN THE CHURCH

1. They criticize everything that is put forward in your favor.
2. They don't see anything good that comes out of what you do and say.
3. They seek every opportunity to not only pull you down, but to make sure you will not rise again, forever.

8. Ibid., 94.
9. Ibid.

4. They stick various true or untrue negative labels on you to make their picture vivid, and plan to destroy whatever you build.
5. They are not predictable in their thoughts and actions. When you keep quiet they will criticize you for keeping too quiet. When you talk they will say you have not talked properly. They are your examiners all the time.
6. They oppose you without listening to what you are saying.
7. They are more in number than what you can ever imagine or eventually know.
8. God deals with them in a special way quite differently from the way you would want to deal with them if you had an opportunity. So, concentrate on your work rather than on them because their agenda may not be predictable to you. However, it is always important to know what they are thinking or are up to.

The Lord himself had even stronger opposition than the one we find in today's church. The beauty of it is, is that such opposition never kills the soul, though it can actually destroy the physical aspect of human life or one's morale when it becomes violent. Further, remember the golden promise, "Behold, I will be with you always until the end of the world" (Matt 28:20).

SOME POSSIBLE METHODS OF DEALING WITH OPPOSITION

1. Preempt critical issues or debates before the meeting. This reduces highly charged exchanges that deteriorate or degenerate into unpleasant discussions.

2. Make adequate research on important issues that are likely to be of greater interest to all constituencies of the church or organization.

3. Talk to individual members of the opposition before critical gatherings to study overall perceptions. Record the mood of the likely topical issues. They cannot say all, but you can read between the lines and prepare accordingly.

4. Allow as much room for high-voltage language to clear thick air. Ignore, but understand, provocative language. Accommodate, in order to dismiss its intentions, a disruption of normal business proceedings.

5. Clarify issues to the best of your ability. Remain truthful, honest, and business-focused. Where you are not sure of appropriate explana-

tions, refer the question to others that might help, or simply admit you are not sure. Alternatively, make a commitment to find out.

6. Never allow yourself to sink to their level. Remain aboveboard, even in your use of professional language. Smile if provoked to neutralize negative excitement that leads to embarrassment.

7. If provoked, remain calm. Remember there are many people in the audience who are supporting you but they can't say it for some personal reasons. So don't let them down by losing their confidence in you.

8. Allow as much open debate and discussion as possible on vital issues of importance for the church. Direct the flow of debate, and prune all loose ends of the debate that lead to any form of irrelevance. Dismiss time wasters with dignity.

9. Never use vulgar language under any circumstances. If cornered, allow more time for debate, welcome contributions, and even digression; that allows you time for silent meditation and re-engagement. Never be emotionally charged. When you do that you lose all dignity, integrity, and respect. You will also lose your audience, and may never be able to regain it.

10. Stick to issues that matter. Remain focused and progressive in your approach to addressing issues of critical value for the organization. Control debate with mature caution. Rebuke any obscene or hate language. Smile to diffuse tension. If you can, just be humorous!

11. Never be emotional. Being emotional is a sign of lack of reasoning capacity. You, therefore, compensate that inadequacy with uncontrolled temper. It's a sign of poor leadership skills. Good leaders have great capacity to accommodate emotionally-charged meetings and audiences. You will not solve anything by any loss of temper. If anything, you lose all your respect by saying things that you feel are retaliatory to a provocative situation. Do not say things that you would never like anyone to say to you.

12. Do not criticize your leaders in public. Remember, they too have people who support them whether they are right or wrong. So, if you lose their confidence, you lose their respect as well. Your work will suffer unnecessarily. You can avoid this loss by maintaining a professional posture.

Prayer: Merciful Lord, please can you turn my problems into blessings? Change my curses into promises of hope? Transform my enemies into friends? Give my enemies more life so they can experience your love and care? Amen.

15

Professional Conduct for Pastors

MEANING OF PROFESSIONAL CONDUCT

PROFESSIONAL CONDUCT REFERS TO the way an individual who occupies a public office behaves in public or private life. This relates, for example, to how a pastor manages his image in the eyes of the public, his family, and the church at-large.

DRESSING CODE FOR PASTORS

A pastor is a church leader in the community and his or her dress code must communicate respect, dignity, and integrity. Church leaders anywhere in the world make an impression through their dress code. They are also judged by their dressing. Many church members imitate their dress code. So proper dressing is an important aspect of professional conduct for the pastorate. It must not be underestimated.

While there is no prescribed dressing code for all pastors at all places in all times, the golden rule for clergy dressing is to be presentable all the time. You carry the image of God in every aspect of your life. Dress professionally as a way of respecting yourself and those who look at you in high esteem. Do not let them down by being shabby. Be friendly to a mirror or looking glass every time you are about to appear in public. There must be a mirror in every pastor's office; if not, try to improvise. Do not take things for granted. When preaching always put on a clerical robe in case you forget to tidy up or button your clothes. These things will get you to lose your image a lot faster than a poor sermon. Once your image is gone you will never regain it.

SPEND MORE TIME WITH GOD

One of the most powerful weapons for any serious pastor to conquer the devil and excel in one's work is the power of prayer. The pastor needs time alone with God. Never underestimate this. Spend quality time with God and you will reap the results that can always amaze you. Prayer means communicating with God at a deeper and individual level. Prayer is very personal. When we walk, sing, breathe, drive, or even sit by ourselves, we can be praying. Prayer makes you feel the presence of God. Prayer is not making noise to other people. There is no such thing as a good prayer. Prayer is praising God, asking God for something, telling God something. If you are normal, you would want to know if the person you are talking to is listening or has heard what you said. Fortunately, God knows what we ask from him before we even say it. God listens, hears, and responds to our prayers as he did in the case of King Hezekiah (Isa 38:1–8) or Cornelius or the children of Israel in the wilderness. In prayer we weaken the devil and gain strength to move forward with life even if all situations around us seem to be negative. Do not pray as a duty. Pray because you feel you need to talk to someone important. In life there are some people who are not worth talking to because they discourage you. God is not like that. He is always there for us, especially in times when we are weak, frustrated, spiritually down, unmotivated, and feeling deserted.

MANAGE YOUR INNER CIRCLE WITH GREAT CARE

No matter how bad any pastor can be he has his own closest friends in any congregation. They appear from shared personal and professional interests. Such friends must be people who are led of the Holy Spirit, and their life and work in the church bear witness to this. In any congregation naturally there are people who identify with the interests of the present pastor. Such interests may be professional, pastoral, personal, or none of these. Naturally there is no human being who lives like an island. We all belong somewhere or identify with certain people. The Lord Jesus himself had his own inner circle of three men: Peter, James, and John. They felt closer to him than the rest of the twelve disciples, and Jesus felt closer to these three than to the rest. Part of the reason why they were closer to the Lord than the rest is that they understood with deeper insight what he represented. The other reason is that they supported him in his work perhaps more readily than the others. We have no record of the others feeling jealous about the Lord's closeness to these three than to the rest of them. This pattern of workmanship must govern today's church. The pastor can have an inner circle, but the circle must be composed of people who are prayerful, God-fearing and, most importantly, people who are truthful. They must not prevent other people to have access to the pastor. Instead, they must facilitate it. They must encourage other people to like the pastor as they do. They must never over-protect the pastor or let him fall into traps set for him by the devil. The major duty of the inner circle is to be the pastor's prayer partners. God chooses these people for the pastor. They feel in their souls that they must join the pastor, or him join them, to fast or pray for something. They take an extra mile in prayer with him. When it comes to giving time, wealth, service, prayer, and presence, they stand with the pastor supporting him at every stage of the way in the work of God.

AVOID TALKING BADLY ABOUT OTHER PASTORS AND LEADERS

There is no pastor who is perfect. Neither is there any individual. We all compliment each other. Never talk badly about your colleague. Doing so is a sign of a serious lack of professional ethics. If you want your congregation to lose confidence in you, then talk badly against your colleague. No matter how bad any person can be, he can always have a good side of him than can benefit other people. Build on what your colleague has done. Correct his mistakes in love and the congregation will respect you and the church, as well. If you have a lot of interest in other people's failure, it means you are a very bad steward of God's church. Bad stewards in the church today destroy the kingdom of God while they attempt to glorify themselves. We must build on each other's work. Where you feel your colleague has done harm to the church approach him in love and talk about the issues; never go to a third person. A third person might be a lot more unwise than yourself! So talk as children of God and be good stewards of the church of God. Be a good steward of your words and thoughts. Be a good steward of senses. This keeps you spiritually alive.

CONTROL YOUR TEMPER

When you are a pastor you are a public figure. People learn from you every day. They learn self-control, disciplined life, good speech, self-respect, and the respect of others from you. Respect other people the way you would want them to respect you. If you call other people foolish or stupid or any other vulgar term, you show how unprofessional you are. In fact they can use worse terms on you than the ones you use against them. This is what bad temper is about. When tempers flare at a church meeting, people show how they can reduce themselves to lesser than human beings, failing to reflect God's image in their speech and conduct.

But how can one go around the problem of temper? When you are angry shorten your speech. This will help you save face after letting out words you would not say when not angry. Remember, once you say unacceptably bad words to another person you cannot unsay them. If they damage the other person you would have destroyed his personality and image. In legal terms you will have defamed that person. There is no amount of money that can remove the damage. Would you like it if other people did the same to you? The pastor must be a very good example of love, tolerance, forgiveness, patience, perseverance, mature conduct, self-control, and respectful speech even when angered or unacceptably provoked. You must make a difference. Do not be emotional. Rather, be factual and remain focused. When you do that you weaken the devil.

POSITIVE SELF IMAGE

Self-image[1] or self–concept or mental self-portrait refers to the way an individual sees himself. Any person with a healthy and positive self-image tends to be out in front in the race of life. If you hate yourself, then you see and feel everyone hates you. If you see yourself as stupid, chances are that you think the world sees you as a stupid person. Or if you see yourself as a beggar, it is likely that you think the rest of the people around see you as a beggar. This type of self-image influences our social life, pastoral work, and spiritual life, as well as our relationships with other people. As human beings we have terrible weaknesses or sins or made bad mistakes in life. Some or most of the times these negative portraits or experiences influence the way we see ourselves. They distort our self-image. To get rid of this negative self-image we must see ourselves as God sees us. We are created in the image of God and all other ways of seeing us must be anchored on this premise. This way of looking at oneself helps us to reimagine the human person. See yourself as God sees you. See yourself as the right image of God, great as he is, be confident and believe in what you do as a successful person: lovable,

1. Mcdowell, *Building Your Self-Image*, 19.

worthy, competent, sinful by nature, but redeemed and reconciled to God through his abundant and overflowing grace. Never spend the majority of your time with people who discourage you or tell you about your weaknesses without attempting to appreciate your strengths.

Neither should you spend most of your time with those who rejoice in your shortcomings and whose value judgments demoralize you all the time. If this happens, turn your weaknesses into sources of strength to succeed in life. Focus on building strengths.[2] An inadequate self-image robs you of your potential to succeed in life. Your self-image must communicate security, success, and confidence. If you have a poor self-image, you create what you fear. You get cheated because you expect it always to happen. You become suspicious because you are not confident in yourself. If you see yourself as a failure, you will find some way to fail, no matter how hard you want to succeed; but if you see yourself as capable of succeeding in life, surely you will face life with confidence. It is important for every pastor to have a positive self-image. If you see yourself as God sees you, then you are the right person for the right job as a pastor. Success is in your hands as your mind is part of what God has instructed, to bring good news to the world for the salvation of humankind.

DEVELOP AND SUSTAIN A POSITIVE ATTITUDE

Attitude is how a person is[3] or feels about himself or other people. This leads to how one behaves or acts. A positive attitude leads to success while a negative attitude is one sure way of failing. Pastors must have a positive attitude with their work in their church and its entire operating system. For any pastor the following guidelines may be very helpful in the creation of a positive attitude towards yourself and other people:

1. Be prayerful. Prayerfulness leads to prosperity in all aspects of life.
2. Make the bible your spiritual manual for life. It provides you with fullness of life.
3. Consult the constitution of your church from time to time.
4. Be in regular communication with your supervisor on matters of ministry and even personal life.

2. Zenger and Folkman, *Handbook for Leaders*, 45.
3. Maxwell, *21 Indispensable Qualities of a Leader*, 197.

5. Share your joys and miseries with your supervisor as a way of getting rid of tension.
6. Have regular meetings with your leaders to check progress of the work of God in your custody.
7. Visit the men, women, and youth fellowships from time to time to pray and fellowship with them.
8. Spend quality time alone, and also with God, at regular or irregular times.
9. At funerals never preach or walk the deceased into heaven or hell; preach to the living and give them hope. Do not cause more pain to the bereaved by showing that you are angry with death, rather prepare everyone for that day so that they can accept it with the joy of eternity that awaits children of God.
10. At weddings or funerals do not repeat the same messages.
11. Welcome all visitors to the parsonage with a happy face and attitude.
12. Make home visitations regular. There is no substitute for this responsibility.
13. Have a vision for your congregation and share it with the leaders and members. Have them walk with you in that vision.
14. Be innovative, creative, and diplomatic in your pastoral work.
15. Be approachable and sociable.
16. Honor your calendar and program as laid down.
17. Pastor to the needs of all under your pastoral supervision, not just your friends or relatives or those who talk good of you.
18. Do not be fond of comparing the previous congregation with the present one. Accept the new order. This habit creates an impression that seems to suggest that the previous congregation was better than the current one. Not many people are comfortable with that comparison.
19. Do not be jealous of other persons' success. Compliment them if they do well in life.
20. Create team spirit with all leaders in the congregation.

21. Be simple and approachable.
22. Maintain a good working relationship with your leaders.
23. Don't correct people in public unless you have no other way of avoiding such a correction. Again build their confidence by praising them in public.
24. Talk to a problem person in public; he will appreciate it and learn faster without resisting.
25. Plan your sermons, and never preach to people but share your understanding of the word of God. Aim to glorify God and not yourself.
26. Take a rest when it is due. Do not force yourself when you feel you need some rest in terms of a day off or annual leave.
27. Create some time off with the family. Do not deny them free time to relax. Remember, to your family you are not a pastor but a parent.
28. Read signs of the times; if you feel it is time to move to the next station or appointment, say so first before the congregation asks you to leave.

Prayer: God, provide me with an image worthy of your calling.
Change my image of hopelessness to one of inspired hope.
Let those who despise me see how almighty you are through
the works of power and faith that you do through me, a weak
vessel of honor. God, are you hearing me? Amen.

16

Cost of Administration[1]

When you become a leader in the church there are advantages that come with the promotion as well as hidden costs that you incur along the process. The costs are challenging and everlasting, but the way you manage them makes a difference. Most, if not all, of the costs have been paid for by Christ already and a prayerful life serves as a reminder.

SELF-SACRIFICE

Every administrative post has costs, some of them hidden. An administrator goes through some very difficult situations, which other people will never come to realize unless they, too, become administrators.

Self-sacrifice is the cost of being a leader, which must be paid, not at the end of every month like most bills are payable, but every day. This is so because "He laid his life . . . and we ought to lay down our lives for the brethren" (1 John 3:16). If we are children of God, we cannot evade the cross, for evading the cross means losing our leadership. The ministry of pastoral administration is a challenge. Be prepared to sacrifice your own resources and time for less remuneration.

Consider this: whoever wants to hold the first positions among you must be everybody's slave. "For the Son of man did not come to be served, but to serve, and to give his life as a ransom" (Mark 10:44–45).

Consider what the apostle Paul says:

> We are pressed on every side by troubles, but we are not crushed and broken. We are perplexed, we don't give up and quit. We are hunted down, but God never abandons us. We get knocked down, but we get up again and keep going. Through suffering, these bod-

1. Sanders, *Spiritual Leadership*, 104–112.

> ies of ours instantly share in the death of Jesus so that the life of Jesus may also be seen in our bodies. Yes, we live under constant danger of death because we serve Jesus, so that the life of Jesus will be obvious in our dying bodies. (2 Corinthians 4: 8–11).

At the same time God does not allow us to face problems for which he would fail to give us the strength to conquer. Indeed, you must feel the apostolic way that "I can do all things through Christ who gives me strength" (Phil 4:13).

LONELINESS

The moment I was appointed a district superintendent I lost all my friends. They assigned me a new set of friends. I became lonely. I had to find new friends within the cabinet. The cabinet was composed of new sets of variables. Those who were older than me knew each other from their primary or secondary school days; other sets were familiar with each other from their days in seminary. Yet, other sets from the small cabinet of only twelve came from the same rural homes; they grew up together, so for them the invitation to cabinet was just a reunion. Other dynamics were always at play. Whether we like it or not, these dynamics manifest themselves in the way we make decisions in running the church or any other organization to which we belong. But I guess Christ is far above all these cultural, tribal, regional, friendly, collegial, and political interest groups. He invites us all as administrators, leaders, or managers of the church to rise above these low levels of operation to a much higher professional standard which reflects spiritual maturity and reputation.

Consider Moses, the great leader of Israel—he was a loner. He paid the price of leadership: alone on the mountain, alone in the plain, alone being criticized for all, and being misunderstood. He was, alone, blamed for all that went wrong. He, alone, was expected to have all the answers to people's complaints.

Consider the prophet Enoch. He was a loner. But he persevered. When you are lonely in pain, thought, fear, despair, frustration, and uncertainty, God will be very close to you.

Consider the man of God, the loneliest of all, Jonah. But he moved on with the message of judgment.

What about Paul himself, the slave of Christ? He was whipped for believing in the gospel but never gave up. That is the uniqueness of administering the church and business of God.

PHYSICAL AND SPIRITUAL FATIGUE

One of the worst challenges of administration is physical and spiritual fatigue. Physical fatigue is whereby you get tired to the extent that you feel emotionally spent; your body refuses to respond to any further physical tasks you may want to do. If you continue to go on working in this state, then you will just be doing it for people to see that you are present. If it is a meeting, you will be attending it just as a duty. If it is a revival, you will be present just because you have to be there. Then you will be wasting time!

Spiritual fatigue is whereby you feel spiritually exhausted. If you enter a revival in this state you will just be making noise during prayer instead of praying. Or, alternatively, you will just close your eyes and your mouth, as well as your mind, to block out all communication with God during prayer. There will be no communication whatsoever because, spiritually, you are suffering from fatigue. To avoid this, the pastor must take time to rest and refresh his mind.

Remember that all human beings suffer wear and tear just like tires on a vehicle. When we work we get tired and must therefore rest. The Lord himself rested a) at the well of Jacob (John 4:6), b) at the back of the boat: "Let's cross over to the other side of the lake." So they got into a boat and started out. On the way across, Jesus lay down for a nap, and while he was sleeping the wind began to rise . . . The disciples woke him up, shouting, "Master, master, we are going to drown" (Luke 8:22–24), and c) "Let's get away from the crowds for a while and rest" (Mark 6:31) and "They left by the boat for a quieter spot" (Mark 6:32). Rest is a critical aspect for any administrator or leader to observe. What time of the year do you take your day off and annual leave? Think about your health, your family, and your spiritual refreshment.

CRITICISM

There is no leader in the world who is immune to criticism or exempted from it. The way he reacts to criticism is what matters. All leaders need to learn something from their critics. Respond with a positive attitude. Do not be forced to lose focus of what you are supposed to do. Do not criticize your criticizer. Instead, teach him by turning his curse into a blessing or an asset by turning negative aspects of the criticism into positive thought. Or ask that person to answer his criticism. Or be honest with the questioner; tell him or her you don't have an answer for that question, if you don't have it. Or ask if anyone from the floor can answer on your behalf.

Remember, all administrators have people who criticize them in the course of their work. Some critics are very good, others are not constructive, yet others still criticize you for the sake of it. All of them are good for your administration because they keep you going. The bible says it all works well for the good of those who love the Lord (Rom 8:28).

REJECTION

All leaders face rejection in one way or another in their course of doing God's work. There are different forms of rejection that occur depending on the type of administration one is doing. The most common reason for people to reject their pastors or leaders is that at one stage or another he will rebuke them or simply challenge them. This will cost you an appointment. For example, if you preach about adultery, corruption, bribes, extra-marital relations at work, fornication, money laundering, borrowing money without the possibility of paying back, divorce, and all things they classify as sensitive then you invite their rejection. But consider what titles the Lord himself gave to the Pharisees: He called them a brood of vipers and white washed walls. At one time he told them it would be easier for a camel to enter through the hole of a needle than for any of them to enter the kingdom of God. They rejected him and condemned him to death. Indeed, he died to save us. How much more for those who are called his children?

PRESSURE

God's work is full of physical and emotional pressure. Physically, such pressure can cost you life. If you work without rest, you get stressed and eventually lose sleep. That may affect your eating habits. A lot of pressure may result in some kind of illness. The only way to cope with professional pressure is to take time off and rest for a while. Take time out for a retreat from your personal relationship with God and with other people around you. In life and ministry never take anything personally. Church work is God's work not your own work. God wants to achieve his goal to save humankind through you and not the other way round. It's not necessary for you to give in to the social pressure emanating from what people are saying about you, rather worry about what God is saying to you. That's all.

Spiritual pressure relates to periods when you feel very low spiritually. It seems as if the communication channel between you and God is closed or very bumpy or cloaked with potholes or just blocked. And yet you feel God must be responding to your prayer requests. At church you pray for things that never get answered. You pray for a child who dies the next day. You marry people who divorce in less than two years in their marriage. This frustrates your spiritual efforts to be aboveboard in terms of what the congregation must achieve.

The only way to cope with spiritual pressure is to take a spiritual retreat. You rest physically while in meditation.

> *Prayer*: My Father, I am lonely, nowhere, stranded, in confusion and have lost hope as this work is most difficult. Where are you, Lord? Come by and comfort me. The challenges of my work are overwhelming. Help me out, I beseech thee. I trust your presence makes a difference. Forgive my mistrust. Amen.

17

The Pastor's Wife

ROLE OF THE PASTOR'S WIFE

In the work of the church, the pastor's wife is a key person. She needs to be a person of noble character, dignified, temperate, and faithful in all things (1 Tim 3:11). She needs to be hospitable and not a difficult person. This does not mean that she has to be an "angel." She is part of the team running the affairs of the congregation, together with the pastor. A lot of adjusting is required on her part, as well as on the part of the pastor for both to work as a team. But, most important, a pastor's wife cannot fulfill her purpose unless she is in a relationship with God.[1] The pastor's wife herself must also understand that she is a unique person.[2] Unique means that she is expected to be exemplary in everything all the time. She is a role model for other spouses in the church and community, just like the pastor. The pastor's wife is like no other person in the congregation and, as a result of this, her talents, abilities, and gifts can never be the same as those of another pastor's wife.[3] She must be understood the way she is. So, it is a mistake to compare her with another pastor's wife. She must be herself. She can develop supportive friends in the church without excluding others. But her best friend must be her husband.[4] But it is also fine for the pastor's wife to have a friend she can unload any bitterness or animosity or any burdensome issues on; and this person may be another pastor's wife in another congregation, if possible.[5]

1. Munroe, *Understanding the Purpose and Power of Woman*, 99.
2. Anderson, *Effective Pastor*, 79.
3. Ibid.
4. Ibid., 81.
5. Ibid.

In addition, it helps if she were never to behave in a strange way in terms of language, temperance, etiquette, dressing, and general appearance. Just as they are one flesh, a pastor and his wife must be consistent in their statements, life style, and attitude towards the church and the membership. Supporting each other is, therefore, very important in ministry. In the context of the church, and possibly in many other organizations, a pastor's wife is a key person in the success or failure of any member of the clergy.

The bible tells us that God planned it this way: "It is not good for the man to be alone. I will make a helper suitable for him" (Gen 2:18). All other helpers may be fine, but they may not be the most suitable. Or, they are helpful but not in a suitable way. Suitable here means she is in a special relationship with the pastor and with God to an extent that she must be honest and truthful with her spouse in good and bad times. In and out of season she must tell her spouse if things are not right in the interest of the church, but using constructive language. As Adam was taken from the ground to work the ground, so was Eve taken from Adam to help him (Gen 2:7; 2:22).[6] Consider the role of Abraham's wife in relation to the man of faith, Abraham. Their home was very hospitable. The woman in Proverbs 31 is most helpful. She takes care of the family, buys a field, and looks after the poor as she is clothed with strength.[7] She is a wife of noble character. She is able to do many things at the same time[8], which is a sign of hard work. Women are gifted with the ability to do several things at one time, better than men. As mentioned in the text, the woman is able to buy a field order household affairs, be involved in trading, all while displaying wisdom and showing compassion.[9] She is involved in multiple tasks and does them successfully.[10] For research, six men and six women were tasked to do the same functions in the same environment as follows: wash up, brew coffee, make toast, scramble eggs, take a phone message, and iron a shirt in a limited time. The result was: men failed. For the women, it was a walkover.[11] A woman thrills man and has the power and strength to attract and stimulate him (Gen 2:23).

6. Benton, *Gender Questions*, 53.
7. Ibid.
8. Ibid.
9. Ibid., 54.
10. Ibid.
11. Ibid.

God made woman to be the glory of man (1 Cor 11:7). She can take care of the most difficult man in the world, as reflected in the story of Abigail in the Old Testament (1 Sam 25). In the New Testament we learn that women from the time of Jesus were ever helpful as we read: "After this, Jesus traveled about from one town and village to another, proclaiming the good news of the kingdom of God. The Twelve were with him, and also some women who had been cured of evil spirits and diseases: Mary (called Magdalene) from whom seven demons had come out; Joanna the wife of Cuza, the manager of Herod's household; Susanna; and many others. These women were helping to support them out of their own means" (Luke 8:1–3).

In the same way, the pastor's spouse can be very helpful in the work of the church. Spouses that fail to help in a suitable way may find this text somewhat challenging. In normal circumstances, the pastor's wife can be a very good source of constructive criticism of her husband's preaching, administration, caregiving, and counseling. She is a point of encouragement and comfort when the work of ministry becomes very difficult. She is part and parcel of the ministry. Although she is not paid by the church for her services, in some denominations she may get appointed by the bishop for women's work alongside her husband. In other denominations she also becomes a pastor by virtue of her husband's calling and appointment. This positions her in a special place of leadership in the church. In some instances, she automatically becomes the chairperson of the women's society. Spouses of those in other professions are fairly free in terms of spousal responsibilities relating to their professions. For example, the manager of a company can afford to miss a meeting where he is required to give a speech. A government minister can afford the same. A medical practitioner or surgeon or chief or teacher can have their spouses absent at a gathering without much hassle. For the pastor, it is not only difficult but it is unacceptable. It is unacceptable for two reasons. First, the pastor must practice what he preaches. God notices the importance of a woman in the life of a man as noted in Genesis 2:18. Companionship in marriage is God's plan for human existence. Man and his wife are the company designed in the scheme of God's economy. In his sight man and woman in marriage are one flesh (Gen 1:24, Matt 19:5). In God's plan for marriage when people get married they must not be separated by anyone: "let no man put asunder" (Matt 19:6). So, marriage is for love, companionship, fellowship, and belonging. The way the pastor relates to other women in the church and in society is watched more by all than the way any other professional would be. The pastorate is a more sensitive office than that of any other person in society by virtue of the call to serve God after having been set apart for that purpose. For that reason, the pastor's wife is a very important person not only in the church, but in society as a whole. If a pastor is found with somebody's wife, the news would not be as shocking or spread as fast as it would be with any other man in society. The news would not last too many years as it would in the case of the pastor. Or if the pastor fights with his wife, the news would be a big story unlike any other couple. This is how married life is important for the pastorate. This is the reason why a pastor's wife is very important. More so, this is part of the reason why the pastor's wife is sometimes addressed as "mother," even by more elderly women in the church when, in fact, she might be much younger than those women and men that address her as such. She is a spiritual mother to all regardless of her age. She must therefore be an exemplary person in speech and practice.

SUPPORT YOUR SPOUSE

1. Spiritual support: There is no other person in the congregation who is most suitably qualified and positioned to pray for and counsel the pastor except his wife. This happens through meditation and fasting. Have time to intercede for him even when preaching, teaching, and chairing crucial meetings. This connection keeps both of you going even if the going gets tough.
2. Emotional support: Stand with your spouse even if it means it's just the two of you on one side. If he is wrong, correct him using constructive language. Pray to God to change what you see as his weaknesses. Do not be offended by his mistakes; rather, develop an assisting attitude. Remember it is all men's weakness not to accept advice from their spouses very quickly because they prefer to know everything. Unfortunately life is not like that.
3. Social support: Support your spouse by being present wherever he is invited to teach, preach, or chair a meeting. Contribute, if possible, by supporting what he will be saying.

Check his dressing before leaving the parsonage. This is important because his poor dressing reflects on what type of person you are. Watch out for his hair, wandering shoe laces, shirt, smelling pair of socks or shoes, uncooperating neck tie, smiling zip, and tight clothes because all these teach, talk, and preach before your spouse says anything. People accept or reject his sermon just after seeing these things, whether you like it or not.

Make sure he eats something before leaving the parsonage because when he is hungry it may affect the way God's work will be done in the field. Or, if he is hungry, when members of the church serve him food, he will eat like he has never seen food in his life, much to your embarrassment!

SPOUSE AND MONEY

1. Avoid borrowing money from church members. You never know what they say about you in your absence in relation to your character and personality.
2. Avoid being bribed by the use of money or goods or groceries. Learn to improve your own life through work and sweat of your own hands.
3. Do not keep church funds in the parsonage. You may be tempted to use them for personal use.
4. Excessive love of money is not encouraged. It damages your spouse's ministry.
5. Be self-reliant by making self-help projects that assist you raise money for your family.
6. Avoid asking for your spouse's pay even when the church delays in the payment of such money.
7. Set priorities together according to the income that comes into the family. Attempt to live within your means. Do not imitate other people because you do not know where they came from in their social life.
8. Train your spouse and children to take care of your in-laws and your own parents without any bias (Exod 20:12).

SPOUSE AND PROPERTY

1. When you are appointed to a church make sure you have a correct inventory of the church property. Take inventory on the first day of arrival so that you do not steal anything by mistake when you leave that station to another appointment. When you leave call the trustees and once again look at the inventory and sign off, without checking on the list what doesn't belong to you.
2. Encourage your spouse to buy your own property. Do not feel satisfied that the church has sofas, curtains, beds, car, fridge, and stove so, therefore, there is no need for you to buy your own. You are fooling yourself. When your spouse dies or retires you will be the saddest person in the community and your members will laugh at you and your children while you become beggars. In turn, you will hate them or the church, but that will not help you in any way nor will it change your situation.
3. Train your children to be responsible with church property or your own property.
4. Avoid giving church property, such as cell phone or car, to your relatives in your absence.
5. Do not be a beggar. A pedestrian never loses respect because he is walking to work while others are driving. If you are offered a vehicle to use for the Lord's work, that is fine, just be responsible. Use it the way you would use your own property. But do not lose your soul for material things that moths destroy.
6. Encourage church members to buy property for themselves. Then, encourage them to do the same for the church.

SPOUSE AND RECEIVING VISITORS

1. The parsonage is every church member's spiritual home, though it is understood as the private home of the pastor. Understand them when they appear as if they are at their own parents' home. Give them food if you have it. Do not feel bad if you fail to feed them because there is nothing to give them.
2. Where a visitor has made an appointment to come to the parsonage avoid a situation whereby the visitor gets into the house while you

are still in the bedroom or elsewhere. Stand by the door while they enter. It is a sign that they are welcome. When they leave, stand outside to bid them farewell. You would love the same treatment when you visit their homes, right?

3. At the parsonage make them feel at home even if things are not right.
4. Teach your members to receive visitors the way Sarah, Abraham's wife, did. In turn, she got good news for her and her husband (Gen 18:1–15).

SPOUSE AND GENERAL ETIQUETTE

1. In every congregation today two thirds of the members learn the following things from the pastor and his wife:

   how to be presentable
   how to react in a crisis situation
   how to respect oneself and others
   how to maintain dignity and integrity
   how to maintain composure
   how to behave in public
   expression of maturity
   how to control pressure
   how to contain excitement
   how to maintain general composure
   how to hold up under pressure
   how to respond to gossip
   how to react to damaging information
   how to protect the church
   how to protect a spouse
   how to relate to in-laws
   how to use acceptable language

2. Be at your best all the time, even in your sleep or when angered or stressed.
3. Avoid bad breath and odor at all costs. Never take off your shoes in public. Take care of your armpits regularly.
4. Be smart: your head, shoes, and posture can tell these very easily.

5. Avoid tight clothes; you may be sending out wrong messages or they may make some people uncomfortable.
6. Avoid too loose or too tight clothes. Inside clothes should keep in their place.
7. Teach your children to dress properly as they are a role model to the congregation and community. If they like clothes that make you feel uncomfortable, discuss this with them and let them have their say in the discussion. Do not be a dictator.
8. Do not overdo anything: reaction, laughing, dozing, talking, giggling, or expressing a point. Overdoing things is a sign of lack of proper professional judgment. People may lose respect for you or honor or professional integrity because of overdoing certain things.
9. Be confident of what you do and say. Weigh your words before you say them out loud because if you say wrong things, it is very difficult to unsay them. It is better to be quiet than to be sorry.
10. Monitor your image always.
11. Self-examine your image, speech, and temper.
12. Correct yourself before other people tell you to.

SPOUSE AND SEXUALITY

Sexuality is a gift from God. Both men and women take equal responsibility to make it work better. A woman needs it just the way the man needs it. But women take more responsibility because they are so special. It has often been said that:

> Whatever you give a woman, she is going to multiply. If you give her sperm, she will give you a baby. If you give her a house, she will give you a home. If you give her groceries, she will give you a meal. If you give her a smile, she will give you her heart. She makes better what is given to her.[12]

This signifies the importance of women in society and marital relations. Marriages, therefore, must be handled with care at both professional and personal levels. At the same time, a woman cannot fulfill her

12. Munroe, *Understanding the Purpose and Power of Woman*, 134.

purpose in life unless she seeks a positive relationship with God.[13] The same applies for men.

1. Sexuality[14] is an integral part of human identity. It is the responsibility of both men and women to understand its role in marriage. It is expressed in a variety of ways, but finds particular expression in intimate human relations. It is a gift of God designed for the purpose of procreation. In addition to finding expression in the physical sense, sexuality in human persons extends to the intellectual, social, emotional, and spiritual dimensions.

2. The Bible says that sex and marriage are God-given gifts and must never be abused (Prov 5:15–21). Sex is a sign that seals a marriage relationship as a covenant. The creator of sex is God, and anything God creates is good.[15] Do not abuse your spouse physically or verbally. This applies to both man and wife. Maturity is very critical in every instance in marriage and sexual life. If any abuse takes place, apology and forgiveness are major aspects of maintaining a marriage relationship.

3. Avoid sex outside marriage as the Bible says it is foolish (Prov 6:23–25). Train your mind to appreciate your spouse as the best ever. If you are constantly working away from home and with people of the opposite sex, provide an impression of disinterest in love relationships that hurt your marriage. Or, if possible, invite your spouse on most of your trips.

4. Train your spouse to understand that sex in marriage is honorable and pure to God and that it deserves commitment (Heb 13:4). Both parties must make a meaningful commitment to it. Do not be selfish, the way you feel is the same way your spouse feels.

5. Preaching is a highly demanding job; understand your spouse on this issue. Do not make unreasonable demands because you may lose the meaning of what it means to enjoy married life.

6. Avoid sharing your marital problems with people whose confidence you doubt. They destroy your marriage without knowing it or intentionally doing it. These people may not even have solutions to your problems.

13. Ibid.

14. For detailed Christian understanding of sexuality, see "*A WCC Study Document*" *on Facing AIDS, the Challenge*: *The Churches' Response*, 30.

15. Cole and Cole, *Unique Woman-Insight.*

7. If your marriage is developing some cracks, pay attention to the possible causes quickly and remedy it. Do not wait to see it crumble. Being quiet is not helpful. Share with God, a confidant or your supervisor in confidence.
8. Avoid pornographic videos, literature, or magazines that might be accessed by your children; it might influence the way they view sexuality at an early age.
9. Avoid cracking sexually suggestive jokes with members of the church. They may misinterpret you. They may laugh but you lose respect forthwith.
10. Do not befriend any particular member of the church more than the rest. Keep a professional relationship with all church members. Maintain a professional distance at all costs.

SPOUSE AND CHILDREN

1. Listen to your children more than anyone else in the church. They see things that they do not agree with. Give them a chance to see things the way they do because they are not you and you are not them. Correct them where you feel they can be made to understand. Teach them to say out loud what they do not like. Do not suppress them because they will grow with those things and say them at a wrong time in life much to the embarrassment of the community. Let them share their joys, concerns, and frustrations with you at a personal level.
2. Pray for each child by name. Take time with each child once a week just to be around with him or her.
3. e fair and firm. You must be consistent when dealing with children; do not change goalposts without explaining things. They will think you are a liar, but they will not tell you that since you are a parent and an adult.
4. If you decide to quarrel or fight with your spouse, do not do so in their sight. You damage them psychologically.
5. Teach them good language. Avoid vulgar language even if you are hurt. Words like rubbish, stupid, idiot, inhuman, you are a dog or a donkey are very damaging to personality images of children. They must never be used in a Christian home. When you use them you

are teaching your children to use them too some time in their life. The way they hurt you is the way they will hurt other people.

6. Take free time or a walk with them, sharing jokes and just laughing about issues that you have read or heard or just witnessed.
7. Never take church business home from the office. Doing this is not a sign of being committed to church work or to God; rather, it is sign that your idea of rest is faulty.
8. Encourage your spouse to take off days and annual leave when they are due. Teach the congregation to understand and appreciate this practice. The pastor will burn out if he does not take a rest.

SPOUSE AND THE EXTENDED FAMILY

1. Respect both your spouse and extended family unconditionally. Do not provide the extended families with groceries privately as this may damage your relationship beyond repair or it may create unnecessary tension.
2. Do not talk bad about your spouse with your parents or relatives. You damage your marriage beyond repair because when it improves it may not always be possible for them to convene in order to correct the records.
3. Encourage each other to pay off outstanding bride wealth if not yet done. This may create relationship problems in due course if no sufficient attention is paid to it in time.
4. Invite the in-laws to your house from time to time. Be happy about their presence. Avoid being moody as you may send undesirable messages.
5. Attend to their needs without delay. Do not wait for them to call you.
6. Show interest in them and their life.

WHAT MAKES A GOOD PASTOR'S WIFE?

The word "good" here, in relative terms, means acceptable. It does not mean perfect. The pastor's family must be a good role model for all other families. It's a thing to pray about. There is a Shona cultural proverb, which emphasizes the importance of women in family life, perhaps in a fundamental way, which says, "*musha mukadzi*" (a wife makes a good home). It does imply that a home without a wife is not a good home.

1. Being a committed spiritual mother of the congregation, and your own family, is very critical for any pastor's spouse. You must fit into this description or you are a complete mismatch with your husband. God will not make you a suitable helper if your attitude does not accept this arrangement.
2. Being tolerant: When people wrong you, take it that they must be forgiven just the way you want to be forgiven. There are ten smart things a woman can do to build a better life[16] which are: create free space for yourself by taking off from a heavy and stinging schedule; manage your emotions well; be in self control; live generously by giving to charity or God; resolve relationships on time before they deteriorate into crises; accept yourself as you are; conquer discontentment; offload stress; plug yourself into people and to God so you can feel their love, encouragement, and be known by them; and understand God's grace to be abundant for you now and forever. That way you will understand yourself to be a worthy person before God and other human beings.
3. Being reliable: People know that when they hear something from you it is definitely not a lie when traced back to its truth.
4. Understanding when dealing with the public. You cannot please everyone you work with. Those that disagree with you must know that you do not hate them simply because they disagree with you.
5. Allow people to talk about you without you saying bad things about other people.
6. Be a good example of what it means to be a mother and wife. Mothers are known for their patience, gentleness, tolerance, and loving attitude—as well as having control of their tempers because of their nurturing abilities for babies and adults too.
7. Being compassionate. Do not enjoy the misery of other people; you will not gain anything from it except selfish unlasting mental excitement.

16. Carter, *10 Smart Things*, 10.

8. Dress properly. Do not let inside clothes hang inappropriately or be seen through. Lose buttons, shoelaces, and tight clothes make life uncomfortable for other people.
9. Convince yourself to be smart and presentable all the time. If you decide to wear makeup, let it be not overdone. The layers must be comfortable with your conscience. Check with your spouse.
10. Be the best dressed person in the congregation all the time. Check with your spouse whether your dressing suits the occasion. Do not put on nightwear inappropriately. Funerals and weddings have their own form of dressing. Informal occasions command their form of dressing. Remember when you put on something odd, the whole gathering or audience will talk about you for some time even after the gathering. You can avoid this ahead of time.
11. Be less talkative and more action-oriented. Most people in the church are very good at talking objectives and plans. Very few are action-oriented. The reason for this is that it is not hard to talk, but very hard to act on what has been planned. Make a difference!
12. Refrain from gossip. Gossip is venomous. It is never constructive. It seeks to destroy lives, property, and God's image in humanity. Gossip is dangerous and treacherous, as well. It must be the last thing a Christian should do, if ever!
13. Be accommodative to all rich and poor in church and the community. Most people, unlike the Lord Jesus, want to be associated with wealthy people, or the learned, or the most popular. A good pastor must accommodate all people. Touch their lives in a special way. Make an impact in their lives. God will bless you for that.
14. Never be away from the family for long, and be helpful to all those who you come across. Make a difference in their lives.
15. Be innovative in order to help the family realize that incomes sustain the family in a meaningful way. Teach the women the same skills to sustain their families.
16. Lead the women of the congregation in their spiritual life by knowing each one of them by name and understand each of them in a personal way.

17. Keep a professional distance from interest groups that may want to be closer to you than the rest of the women in the church and community.
18. Be very clear of the work of the pastor and respect him as such, and realize the importance of supporting him for the good of the work of God.
19. Never rebuke your spouse in public no matter how bad things may have become. Most people learn better from their mistakes when rebuked in private and with the use of loving and constructive language.
20. Be self-reliant and do not beg from the church or members of the church and community. It if fine if they give you clothes, food, or money on their own, but never beg! You should also donate to them as a gesture of good will. God will bless you for that.
21. Never be late for anything, especially where you are required to be as a pastor's spouse. Remember, you embarrass your husband very much when you are late to a place where you are supposed to be the first person to get there. Do not make life difficult for other people by coming late. If you are ill or delayed, communicate it in a professional manner.
22. Praise your spouse and your children when they do well and share your concern in good language when something you feel is wrong takes place. You rebuke them with respect. The same for church members; do not shout at them or lose your temper. Correct them in love. They will learn better that way.
23. Always maintain a sense of humor. Laugh where it's appropriate and show resentment where it deserves. That keeps you going. You become abnormal if you laugh inappropriately or make a joke that sticks.
24. Do not overeat when you are given food. Be an average person. Consider others when dishing your plate. Take small amounts to start with to make sure everyone has a chance to have something in their plate. Then you can always go for another dish if all others have had their share. You will naturally feel bad if others fail to have food while your plate is overflowing. It's a matter of conscience! If you are invited to a party, eat something before you go there to avoid performing abnormally at the table.

25. Never pretend to be someone that you are not because other people may be working hard to be like you.
26. Be forgiving all the time. If you are not happy or comfortable about something, say it before it eats you up. But use good language that earns you the respect of others, including your spouse and your children.
27. Maintain your self-image all the time. Thank God he made you the way you are. Do not pretend to be what you are not. The world enjoys its beauty because you are different from anyone else. You add color and variety to God's artistic hand.
28. Be God-fearing all the time. People who fear God find it easy to relate to other persons because when one's relationship with God is right it is very abnormal to have negative relations with other human beings.

LEADING OTHER WOMEN

When leading other women who may or may not be members of the women's fellowship, take note of the following:

1. Incorporate their ideas in your planning of their programs.
2. Involve, also, the less prominent women in the sharing of ideas.
3. Ask some of them who are usually quiet to give their input.
4. Help the most talkative to keep their place in any discussion.
5. Get the elderly to give advice when you plan your work.
6. Help the most wealthy and influential ones to keep their place in the activities of the organization.
7. Do not be bribed into making decisions that benefit a few at the expense of the rest. Accommodate everyone in decision-making.
8. Be careful about a few people who come after a decision has already been made and want to make changes to suit them. They may be an advantage or a disadvantage to your administration. They may keep quiet if things go wrong following their advice to you, or they may praise you if what they advised you become accepted.

9. Be approachable by all, including those who are not thought of as good people—such as those who are not gifted in their character, speech, and attitude.
10. Create discussion space for single mothers. Give them a platform to share their experiences, frustrations, stress, fears, uncertainties, plans, and hopes.
11. Regard everyone as important and different from the rest. Respect them as they are, regardless of social and economic status.

IN YOUR OWN HOME

1. Pray for each child by name for success, good health, wisdom, and vision.
2. Pray for your spouse for wisdom, good health, and happiness.
3. Pray for both of your extended families. Be available to them at all times.
4. Initiate visits to both sets of parents, not just your own.
5. Initiate the buying of presents for your spouse's parents and then your own. Be sensitive. The way you feel about your parents is the way your spouse feels about his or her parents.
6. Do not make negative comments about your spouse's parents or to show dislike for them, even if you pretend to like them later, you will have lost your spouse's respect forever. The way you dislike them is exactly the way he will dislike you, even if you go to bed together. It might turn out to be that he will, in turn, dislike your parents as a silent message that never pronounces itself. The same applies for relatives.
7. Teach your children to love both members of the extended families. If you are biased, then you are a very bad parent. Bad in the sense that when both of you die they may have a difficult time to relate to their relatives.
8. Teach your children to be self-reliant in terms of work attitude. Give them tasks to do on their own. Or ask them at a tender age to make decisions and then guide them. Do not decide things that affect their life all the time. Ask them to be responsible at an early age.

9. Teach your children to say no to things they do not like. That is how the world works. People who were never trained at an early age will be fooled to accept things they do not like in life because the word "no" was not a part of their upbringing.
10. Teach your children self-respect. Never give your children an impression that pastors' families are the poorest in the world. Teach them that being a pastor is a calling and a personal decision to serve the Lord in a special way, and not that you could not find another job on the market. Do not pretend. If you are angry, indicate to them your displeasure. If they are wrong, do not pretend to be happy about them because if you pretend, you send wrong signals to them that everything is always fine even if it is not. These wrong signals will get them to behave inappropriately in the real world. So, there is the popular saying "pastors' children are mischievous." The reason may be that they are caught between a real world and one that pretends the wrong things. Do not teach your children to hide things they are not happy about. Teach them to express themselves and correct their expressions immediately.
11. Never make a negative comment about your spouse that suggests to the children that your husband is foolish, stupid, an evil man, or a demon because they came from him. Find other ways of winning their favor rather than getting them to your side with hate speech. They are innocent as far as your differences as parents may be concerned. The danger of this is that they will behave the same to their children when they become parents. What a world we will have in the future if it is made up of such parents!
12. Never make a vulgar statement in front of children. You are not helping them; perhaps you will be helping yourself empty out, vent out your poison! And never report a child's wrong to your spouse—he becomes the devil of the home. Deal with the problem yourself. That is what motherhood is about. It's not about shifting disciplining responsibility to one parent. Very foolish parents do this.
13. Do not quarrel or fight in front of children. If the devil gets hold of you both, perhaps the bedroom may be suitable for a show-off of such differences. But it is uncalled for. It is uneconomic as far as energy consumption is concerned! Isn't it? There is need for tolerance, patience, accommodating each other in the way you look at

things, respecting one another, and an attitude of learning from each other that must prevail. Attitude is very important for any marriage. It takes a lot of compromises. No marriage is perfect, but all those in it continue daily to grow it to perfection. Those who adopt an attitude of "not with me" will find marriage a very difficult relationship to control. Couples learn from each other every day. Christian parents must talk things over. Never spend the whole day angry, so St. Paul says, (Eph 5:26).

14. Never compare children as better or worse because they are born different. They are as different as their names. They do not have the same talents, weaknesses, or strengths. Respect them as they are even if you know of their differences; it is your own privileged information.

AVOID ANGER BECAUSE OF THE FOLLOWING PROBLEMS

1. Anger can lead to murder (Gen 4:3–8).
2. Anger leads to evil action (Ps 37:8).
3. Showing anger is foolishness (Prov 12:16).
4. Being quick-tempered is foolish (Eccl 7:9).
5. God becomes angry when we are ruled by anger (Amos 1:11).
6. Anger is like murdering someone (Matt 5:21–22).
7. Jesus grew angry at sin (John 2:13–17).
8. Anger can give Satan a place in your life (Eph 4:26–27).
9. Christians should get rid of anger (Col 3:8).
10. Leaders in the church should not be quick-tempered (Titus 1:7).
11. The Bible teaches us to be slow to anger (Jas 1:19).

Anger can lead us to act in ways that God does not approve. For example, in Zimbabwe a Member of Parliament murdered his wife because he found her with another man. This is just the tip of an iceberg. Several stories in the local and international media carry stories of men and women who are led by anger into killing other people because they have failed to control their tempers.

GENERAL ADVICE TO THE PASTOR'S WIFE[17]

1. Avoid criticizing your spouse in public; rather, advise him in good spirit privately.
2. Do not criticize your husband's messages or sermons without offering suggestions for improvement. Motivate him to do better next time. If asked point out, the good points first and then share your ideas on how he can improve next time.
3. Avoid asking for information following any counseling sessions that your husband has done with a member of the church or anyone else. If he feels you need to know, he will volunteer the information at an appropriate time. In return, offer good advice. Avoid torturing your spouse by putting pressure to know what went on during counseling; it is not your business.
4. Keep your home a welcome place for those who come with or without an appointment. Do not keep them standing outside the doorstep. Be sensitive to why they have come. Sometimes just a smile on your face lightens up their day or life. They may just be in need of someone to talk to.
5. On Sundays, before and after worship service, perhaps all the time, be friendly to everyone, not just your special friends. Identify the isolated and make them feel happy just like all other people. This helps them to share if they have some problems.
6. Be a good listener. Reserve comments. If you are not sure of what to say, don't say anything, just show a happy face.
7. Know your church teachings and polity (how the church is organized or run) in case some members will come to you for answers to some questions on marriage, death, or prayer. If you are not sure, be honest and say so or promise to find out.
8. If employed elsewhere, take time to do God's work. God will reward you for it in a special way. If you can't attend a certain meeting due to other work related commitments, feel free to say so rather than force matters. Do not take it as a bother, but a positive challenge with rewarding results at the end of it.

17. Anderson, *Effective Pastor*, 28.

9. On administrative matters of the church or in your family or private life, do not show that you are worlds apart from your spouse. If what you say is very different from what your spouse is saying, one of you might be thought of as a dishonest person. Guard against this by telling the truth. You will earn everyone's respect by being a truthful person.

Prayer: Dear God, make me a good spouse. Fill me with wisdom to provide advice in love. Teach me to be patient. Help me to forgive. Give me the strength to rise early in the morning and talk to you. Amen.

18

Listening to the Holy Spirit

IN ADMINISTERING THE CHURCH in unique and difficult circumstances, we have a promise of the Holy Spirit as our counselor. The most important thing to do is to listen to what God is saying to us through his presence with the Holy Spirit.

WHO IS THE HOLY SPIRIT?

Outside the guidance of the Holy Spirit, the pastor has no life. He becomes an instrument without any sound or substance. He is a vehicle without fuel or a ball without pressure or a hoe without a handle. It must be a challenge for every pastor never to attempt to do God's work without inviting the guidance and presence of the Holy Spirit. A church that has stopped calling and listening to the voice of the Holy Spirit is like a club that has no spiritual values. Such a church is very difficult, if not impossible, to run. Its members come to church for fellowship or nonspiritual business, and they can do that very well, although it will have nothing to do with God. All churches must have the spiritual touch of the Holy Spirit at every level and every stage to avoid mimicking the language of heaven. The leaders of the church must seek truth and humility, with earnest, the face of the Lord and the presence of the Holy Spirit in season and out of season. Pray without ceasing to ask for the presence of the Holy Spirit in the church.

But who is the Holy Spirit? By definition, the Holy Spirit is God. The Holy Spirit is part of the Godhead or the trinity. The Holy Spirit is our comforter. He takes care of us all the time. There is no church worth its name that can survive in the world today without the sustenance of the Holy Spirit. The Holy Spirit is our guide in the present life and the life to come. The church, to be effective today as has always been, has to be an instrument of the Holy Spirit.[1] It is through the Holy Spirit that the church has found its birth and strength. The more the church is evangelical and faithful to its calling and origins, the more it will remain true to itself, and it becomes more relevant to its purpose of existence. At Pentecost the Holy Spirit came down to fill the apostles during a time they were glorifying God. The Holy Spirit comes when the Savior is glorified.[2] In our churches today the Holy Spirit comes when the Lord Jesus is glorified.[3] When the Holy Spirit comes to us we experience joy and power and we become positively influential and useful in the church in very exceptional ways.[4] As would be with God, the Holy Spirit is that which nothing is greater. He is our comforter and counselor.

WHAT DOES THE BIBLE SAY ABOUT THE HOLY SPIRIT?

The Bible is the inspired word of God. The word of God says something about the Holy Spirit. "I will ask the father and he will give you another Counselor, who will never leave you," says the Lord to his disciples. He is the Holy Spirit who leads to all truth. Humankind has never had such a great promise of eternal value. We hear that the world at large cannot receive him, because it is not looking for him. But because those who seek him will find him and he will dwell in them at their request. All churches that are worth their name cannot live outside of the power of the Holy Spirit.

1. The Holy Spirit gave origin to the creation of the universe (Gen 1:26, John 1:1–4). He has the power to create things from nothing, without our help. He is the creative power that gave rise to the origin of the world.
2. The Holy Spirit empowers leaders (Judg 3:10).
3. He teaches us (John 14:25).
4. He guides us (John 16:3).
5. He empowers us to be witnesses (Acts 1:8).
6. He dwells within us (Rom 8:11).
7. He sanctifies us (Rom 15:16).
8. He opens our spiritual eyes (1 Cor 2:10).
9. He gives us salvation (Titus 3:5).

1. Sues, *New Pentecost?*, 16.
2. Ibid.
3. Tozer, *Counselor Straight Talk*, 3.
4. Ibid.

10. He gives us protection from sin.
11. He provides us the power to discern between good and bad.
12. He takes care of us in this life and the afterlife.
13. He gives us power to love and to do God's will.
14. The Holy Spirit leads us to know the truth and to live by it.

HOW DOES THE HOLY SPIRIT MANIFEST IN THE CHURCH TODAY?

There are several ways in which the manifestation of the Holy Spirit is found in the church today. But it is important for those who wish to experience the power and presence of the Holy Spirit to first open up their spiritual eyes for this miracle to happen. The Holy Spirit manifests in the church today in the following ways:

1. Obedience to God's will: The prophet Isaiah, in a remarkable and dramatic turn-around after his spiritual encounter with God, obeys to be sent to redeem society from sin (Isa 6:1–8). He says, "here I am send me." God's call is irresistible. Thus, obedience in doing God's will is an indelible mark of a Christian.

In the church today, people who personally rise to have extra responsibilities, in addition to tithing, are obedient servants of the Lord. They allow themselves to be sent to do God's will. They will do what the Holy Spirit tells them to do. If the Holy Spirit tells them to pay the pastor's salary for a month or half a year, they will obey. One woman bought the church office a new office chair, a fax machine, and two telephone receivers. She obeyed what the Holy Spirit told her in terms of her service to the church. Another man and his wife paid the allowances for all of the six top leaders of the church, and a new suit to the bishop of the church. Another couple bought a car for the pastor, while another, in fact, donated furniture.

2. Listening to God: The Holy Spirit came into the Lord Jesus at his baptism and confirmation was made that he was the son of God and that we should all listen to him (Luke 3:21–22.) The Holy Spirit can manifest himself in natural phenomena, such as a burning bush in the case of the great Israelite leader Moses, or a dove in the case of the Lord's baptism, or wind in the case of the creation narratives, or flames or tongues of fire in the case of the Pentecost event. Listening to the voice of the Lord in all cases is very important for all believers who communicate with God in unique ways.

3. Performing miracles of healing, preaching good news to the poor, proclaiming freedom of those imprisoned physically and spiritually, recovery of sight to the blind, and release of the oppressed are all manifestations of the presence of the Holy Spirit in the church or family or community as the Lord says (Luke 4: 16–19). There is no church or individual who can perform these acts without the power of the Holy Spirit.

4. Producing fruits of the Holy Spirit such as love, joy, peace, patience, peace, kindness, goodness, faithfulness, gentleness, and self control all show that the Holy Spirit is manifesting within a family or church or community (Gal 5:22–23). When a Christian does good to all people, the Holy Spirit will be manifesting himself in that person (Gal 6:10).

5. Living as children of the light is a manifestation of the Holy Spirit. "Do not let the sun go down while you hold on to your anger," the apostle Paul says (Eph 4:26). The ability to forgive is a manifestation of the Holy Spirit.

6. The ability to avoid unprofitable talk is a manifestation of the Holy Spirit. Say what is helpful for building up others (Eph 4:29).

WHAT CHANGES CAN THE HOLY SPIRIT BRING INTO OUR LIVES?

When we take time to listen to the Holy Spirit we can hear the secrets of the cross with a keen interest. The Lord gives us holy advice, critical counsel, lasting comfort, inspiring motivation, and meaningful ways of interacting with the people of God in a special way. We can experience change in our lives by listening to the Holy Spirit.

NOTICEABLE CHANGES THAT COME OUR WAY WHEN WE LISTEN TO THE HOLY SPIRIT

Change from hating other people to loving them without conditions.
Change from being boastful to humble.
Change from impatience to tolerance.
Change from greedy of power to sharing of responsibility.
Change from autocratic administration to delegation of authority.
Change from jealousy to the joy of celebrating the success of other people.
Change from influencing people to think negatively or have a low opinion of those who do not seem to like you to talking good of them.

Change from degrading other people to raising them up in prayer and meditation.

Change from being a slave of temper to self-control and spiritual maturity.

Change from a negative attitude towards giving in the church to a blessed hand that gives cheerfully and abundantly.

INVITING AND RECEIVING THE HOLY SPIRIT AS A PERSONAL SAVIOR?

1. Make a personal search for the presence of the Holy Spirit, just the way Nicodemus did (John 3:3–21). When he met, and poured all his spiritual ignorance to the Lord, Nicodemus received a revelation that led to his salvation. He received a rebirth, renewal, and conversion of his heart.

2. Seek a personal encounter with the Lord. When the tax collector Zaccheus fell short, both physically and spiritually, of the glory of God he made a personal move to encounter the Lord. They spoke heart to heart. The Lord knows all those who are short of his presence and when they seek him he will, in turn, invite them to dine with him in their hearts and homes. The church must do this. Individual members of the church of God must do this: seek a personal encounter with the Lord at a personal level.

3. Conduct a self-examination and make a personal decision to accept Christ. The woman of Samaria had cut ties with the Lord and the community. But in a dramatic turn she became the first woman preacher after taking a rigorous conversion discourse with the Lord at the well of Jacob (John 4:15). She says, "Sir, give me this water so that I won't get thirsty and have to keep coming here to draw water." She was saying heal my sinfulness once and for all so that I will not want to sin again.

For all the cases above St. Paul says, "Therefore if anyone is in Christ he is a new creation, the old has gone the new has come" (2 Cor 5:17).

WHAT HAPPENS WHEN WE WALK IN THE SPIRIT?

1. We become capable of loving one another.
2. We will have no problems in relating with other members of the church. We will take our differences to mean a diversity of opinion that helps us to grow spiritually.
3. We will not have problems in tithing as a principle of prosperity. We will, in fact, give cheerfully as the Corinthian church did.
4. We will train our ears to listen only to helpful information that comes our way.
5. We will never entertain any form of grudge with any person whatsoever.
6. We will have no problem in forgiving those persons who wrong us.
7. The spirit of discernment will abide in us.
8. We will never harbor ill feeling or hate that will destroy our lives physically and spiritually.
9. We will not feel evil for other people.
10. We will forever rejoice the success of other people in life.
11. The church will not struggle to get things done through us in the form that the Prophet Isaiah availed himself for the work of God.
12. We will fear God more than we fear human beings.
13. Christ will be the Lord of our conscience all the time.
14. We will walk righteously.
15. God will fulfill his promises to us.

UNFORGIVABLE SINS AGAINST THE HOLY SPIRIT

1. Grieve not the Holy Spirit (Eph 4:30).
2. Lie not to the Holy Spirit (Acts 5:3).
3. Resist not the Holy Spirit (Acts 7:51).
4. Tempt not the Holy Spirit (Acts 5:9–10).

Prayer: Heavenly Father, teach me to listen to you carefully. Counsel my character. Give me a new image. Teach me how to forgive. Help me to walk in the expectation of the Holy Spirit. Clean my heart and personality. Amen.

19

Pastoral Visitation

WHAT IS PASTORAL VISITATION?

Pastoral visitation is the pastor's ministry of making himself present in a situation where a client is in need of care. Church members receive many visitors in their homes every day or week or month or year. What makes your visit to such homes pastoral? Every pastor must ask these questions: Am I making a difference by this visit? What is unique about each pastoral visitation that I make to each home? It must be known clearly that your visit represents God. You must then represent him well in image, speech, and impression. Where do you get the guts to represent other people or interests while on pastoral visitation? Pastoral visitation is the pastor's attendance to the spiritual needs of the family placed under his spiritual care by the church. It is God's visit to the people through his chosen vessel. So during the visit, and beyond it, the person you visit must feel the presence of God in his or her heart and home.

The Bible tells us of a story where three people visited Sarah and Abraham. As this couple's guests, they were given food. Later, during their discussion, it was discovered that they represented God himself. It was a pastoral visitation. They brought good news to this couple that a son was to be born out of their long wait for a child. It was in their favor to host them. All forms of pastoral visitation must bring good news to the client.

WHY PASTORAL VISITATION?

For any person who has accepted Jesus Christ as a personal Lord and Savior, pastoral visitation is very necessary. Even for any person who has a soul, mind, body, and strength pastoral visitation is a desire of the heart because there is no human being who is without needs of the soul, mind, and body. All professional people, and those without anything they can call a profession, have need for a pastoral visit—a visit by a man or woman sent by God to see how they are faring and to share concerns of their life at a very personal level, free of charge. So, all human beings have a heart's desire and spiritual longing for a pastoral visit—a visit into their hearts and homes. We, then, do pastoral visitation for the following reasons:

1. To attend to the spiritual needs of the family of God.
2. To strengthen the faith of the members.
3. To comfort the members after losing a loved one.
4. To pray with the members of the church or community.
5. To counsel with members in stressful situations.
6. To join families in good times such as marriage or any form of celebration.
7. To empathize with clients in times of loss of property or life.
8. To show concern in times of loneliness.
9. To keep members in distressed conditions in spiritual company.
10. To reduce or alleviate grief by being present for the members, to have a shoulder to lean on during crisis.
11. To be a shepherd in and out of season.
12. To provide healing after a family, or personal, dispute or a devastating situation.
13. To create a positive attitude towards the self in members who are facing self-blame.
14. To intervene in the life of those persons facing the edge of depression.
15. To encourage those persons who will have lost hope in life due to circumstances beyond their control.

16. To help families going through divorce or separation cope in their pain.
17. To work with those persons struggling with chronic illnesses accept their condition and to live positively.
18. To help work out ways of saving those persons struggling to come out of drug abuse and alcohol abuse.
19. To help people talk to God even in times of crisis.
20. To counsel those persons facing sexual problems in their life and marriage.
21. To provide counsel to children who have lost one or both parents to HIV/AIDS or through an accident or any form of stressful situations.
22. To create self-confidence in divorcees who have lost hope in married life.
23. To help children who hate their parents understand the role of parenthood, or help parents who hate their children understand the demands of childhood.
24. To attend to the needs of those persons facing denial in real life situations that they may be encountering.
25. To encourage positive thinking in those persons who are facing hopelessness in life.
26. To provide counseling to both adolescence and those retiring who may be facing the challenge caused by these developments.
27. To counsel those persons who have lost a pregnancy or a job or a title or have failed an examination or something dear to them.
28. To encourage those persons who are facing terminal illness.
29. To just be available for the client at a spiritual and professional level, thereby creating lasting spiritual and professional relationships.
30. To show care and concern in any personal or family situation of the client.
31. To represent the church and the image of God at every stage of the visitation.

WHAT MAKES PASTORAL VISITATION EFFECTIVE?

The only thing that makes pastoral visitation effective is the response that comes after, or out of, it. Have you achieved your purpose of the visit? If yes, what are the results of such a visit? Your members obviously do respond in various ways to your visit as a pastor. Some acknowledge it. Others appreciate it in various ways. Yet, some may just cry in your presence. Others will give a testimony later in life or immediately. Some will confess their sins. Much depends on what the purpose is of a particular visit. Pastorally, you must feel satisfied that you have achieved something after the visit. The satisfaction is usually an inner professional and spiritual feeling and a sense of success that accompanies your return from such a pastoral visit. You feel a sense of accomplishment. The following may be some of the results of an effective visitation:

a) an improvement in the situation you addressed
b) positive feedback from the client
c) a follow-up to the situation by the client
d) more clients turning up for pastoral attention on similar situations
e) personal testimony at later spiritual revivals or crusades
f) congregational support by clients to other members of the congregation
g) presents to the parsonage

HOME VISITATION

Home visitation of church members by the pastor is a very taxing responsibility. It is not like reading a book in order to finish it; rather, it is just like starting on a journey the purpose for which is to understand its content. The pastor engages in pastoral visitation in order to minister to the members through care and concern for them. So it must be thorough. The reason for this is that the pastor has to plan, organize, strategize, make it meaningful and acceptable, and fulfill it as planned in terms of time and schedule. There are two types of pastoral visitation. These are general and qualitative visitations.

a) General pastoral visitation

This is the type of visitation where the pastor goes into the homes of the members just to see how they are faring in their spiritual and social life. There is no specific objective except to see where the members are located on his map and to offer general prayers and counsel to them without any major focus. This is most common for pastors who are new appointees to their parishes. For general visitation the pastor can go with someone like his or her spouse or one of the leaders or members of the congregation.

Characteristics of general pastoral visitation

1. It has no specific timeframe within the year or month or week. It can be Sunday after worship or during the week or three months in a year.
2. It may be announced to the whole congregation. This is done to prepare the various families to receive the pastor in their homes. Surprises are very unpleasant for most families. Do not go to any home unannounced. You will embarrass yourself or your host.
3. It must cover every member of the congregation. Do not be selective. Visit all: poor or wealthy, popular or unpopular, young and old, old and new, destitute and physically–challenged, as your conscience tells you.
4. It can be extended to other members of the community who do not come to church depending on the availability of time on the part of the pastor.
5. It has no need for scripture quotation or textual concentration. Your presence is pastoral enough and doesn't need to say anything more. Read the situation as to whether it requires for you to read a scripture passage or sing a full song from your hymn-book.
6. It includes all members of the family at prayer time. Ask for what they feel you must address in your prayer. These prayer requests are critical stages of their spiritual life as a family; therefore, they must be diarized for future follow up and reference.
7. The pastor addresses any issues that are put before him or her for pastoral attention. These are confidential spiritual and social concerns to be raised in your own prayer time at the office or parsonage. Take them seriously.
8. The pastoral prayer is general, depending on the issues given or discerned during discussion.

9. The pastor does not often take notes for further spiritual attention. Issues are dealt with immediately.
10. Referral ministry in the form of writing may not be emphasized.

b) Specific pastoral visitation

This is the type of pastoral visitation that requires special attention, or where the pastor attends to specific pastoral programs of visiting members that have been identified as needing such visits and pastoral care. The pastor may suspend all other schedules and programs and focus on need-based and specialized care. Such visits require special pastoral skills. Examples of such pastoral visits include cases of those who are terminally ill, bed ridden, divorcing, separating, adopting a child, attending a court case that has potential for a prison term, those awaiting trial, those awaiting a medical operation, those who lost a job or a home or retired earlier than they expected, or those who have lost a loved one naturally or through a traffic accident or suicide cases or other causes.

Characteristics of qualitative pastoral visitation

1. Plan what and how to say what you should say before you go. Be engaging. Address the real issues without being general. Remember the question Jesus asked a blind man: "What do you want me to do for you"? He says, "I want to see." The Lord opened his eyes. So be specific.
2. Proper timing must be done before going. Check with the client before you proceed to visit. This is critical because you want to avoid disturbing the peace and quiet moments of your client, especially in the case of those who may have lost loved ones.
3. Overstaying must be avoided. Staying more than the time expected creates an impression that you have nothing else to do, so you decide to kill time that way.
4. Unnecessary frequency often creates lack of purpose.
5. The spirit of discernment must be sought during counseling as you often run short of words to counsel or comfort those in very complicated situations of loss. If the client has many questions that have no answers, do not pretend to have the answers. The Bible, too, does not have these answers. It can give you passages to read when

comforting the client who has lost a loved one, but every situation is unique.

6. Empathize with the client without exaggerating or taking the loss too lightly as an attempt to comfort. If you have examples of similar problems that you have experienced, do not overemphasize them because you do not know what message you may be sending to the client.
7. Two-thirds of your time during the visit must be resorted to listening while the client talks out the problem. Talkative pastors must restrain themselves as much as possible. Less talking is important because it is your presence that allows your client to talk. Your presence is a dramatic demonstration of spiritual solidarity with the client; it is a source of hope, encouragement, and inspiration.
8. One visit may need to be followed by two or three or even more visits to the same client, depending on the situation. Avoid showing an attitude that says the client's situation is too much or too tiring or hopeless, especially for those who are facing a terminal illness.
9. Pastoral prayer must be specific, and scripture readings must be planned to suit the situation.
10. The visitation itself must not be announced to the congregation, especially if it is related to a terminal illness such as HIV/AIDS so as to avoid stigmatization.
11. Keep all matters confidential at all costs. Your spouse is not part of the visitation. Keep things to yourself.

UNPROFESSIONAL CONDUCT DURING PASTORAL VISITATION

1. Do not show, or give an impression, that you are in a hurry to move to the next home or family by cutting the conversation or stopping somebody from crying or emptying what is in his or her life. Let the process go because this is a healing process. Simply provide guidance by asking if you can be allowed to pray.
2. Do not overstay at one family's home, depending on the issues that have brought you to that home.

3. When given food, make a decision to accept or decline. Be reasonable to accept if they insist. Be culturally sensitive.
4. Do not give your client a hard time by being selective in what he or she wants to offer you as food. If you feel you do not want it, be honest. Find a polite way of rejecting it without offending your client.
5. Do not ask for anything to carry home unless they offer it to you. The Lord told the disciples never to carry anything, but accept if given something.
6. Do not be over-excited when given something that you do not have at home, or breathe a sigh of relief openly when offered such a scarce commodity.
7. Do not compare persons and families on the basis of what they have and what they may not have in terms of social status.
8. Do not talk about, or be drawn to talk negatively about, other members while on pastoral visitation.
9. Do not frequent certain homes more than the rest. Give all your members fair amount of pastoral visits and attention.
10. Do not direct events or command the family or person you are visiting, but make professional requests such as "can I kindly ask to make a prayer" or "could you allow me to pray." Do not say to the children "switch off the television." That is very impolite.
11. At a funeral do not be the funeral director, ask if they want any consultation help. This is critical because people become family members before they become church members, so give the family their room to run their affairs. You are there only to give advice and counsel. If they want you to lead in the events, then feel free to do so.
12. Do not be judgmental even if you hate the situation you are facing as a pastor. You are not a judge but a pastor, a shepherd, a care giver—not a care robber. Let them not wish you away but feel your presence alone is their source of comfort.
13. If you want to use the toilet, ask in a professional manner such as "may I be allowed to use your toilet?" Do not say "where is the toilet"?

14. If you visit a couple and one of the spouses is away from home, do not make insulting statements like "these days many couples do not survive away from each other" or "is this the best situation for you"? Make spiritual comments like "the Lord takes care of all situations."
15. Before leaving, kindly ask if you could be allowed to pray. Do not say "I want to pray." During your prayer do not quarrel with God or blame him or the client for a negative situation. Ask for God's guidance and wisdom in dealing with complex situations.
16. Do not direct the client where to sit when praying or direct that you put hands on them; you can still make an effective prayer without touching anyone anywhere. God will still heal or make miracles if he decides to. You do not heal but God does.
17. Do not blame the client for anything he or she shared with you.
18. Keep all matters of professional and pastoral concern in strict confidence.
19. Do not laugh at your client or show such an attitude even if you are told a stupid story that affects your client. Be sympathetic or empathize.
20. Do not over laugh, or over eat or over stay. If you feel that you are being unaccepted, do not respond showing that you are hurt, be professional and act as if all is fine, but pray about it in your heart.
21. If for some reason a certain member tells you not to visit him or her, accept that as a challenge. Maybe you can just phone to say how are you. If that person loses a relative, join others to go and pay condolences and keep a professional relationship with that person. Do not develop a negative attitude towards those persons you feel hate you or just do not like you— it's their choice not to like you! Never say any statements that show you are aware of their hate for you. Just love and work with them as God's people. This is the cost of being a leader— not being liked by all and yet you have to love all.

HOSPITAL VISITATION

Steps taken in preparation for hospital visitation:

1. Identify the individual's first and surname.

2. Identify the ward and bed number.
3. Identify contact number of the client's next of kin and keep in touch.
4. Identify visiting times.
5. Identify the doctor's name.
6. Pray before you leave for this visitation asking the Lord what helpful words to say to the patient.
7. Know what the problem is and pray for that specifically.

UNPROFESSIONAL CONDUCT DURING HOSPITAL VISITATION

When you visit a patient at the hospital:

1. Do not show a sad face. Smile to give hope, life, and encouragement. Never cry at the situation no matter how bad it may be because you are there as a source of courage, hope, and inspiration. Everyone is looking up to you for comfort. Give it to them. Do not fear. If the situation is frightening, ask God to strengthen you. Tell yourself, "I am in charge, God is with me right here."
2. Do not overstay. You strain the patient. The patient needs more time with his relatives and medical staff. You are fortunate that, for professional reasons, you are allowed in the healing ministry of that patient, so do not spoil it.
3. When you ask to pray do not shout, God will still hear you even when you whisper.
4. When leaving, say something to the sister-in-charge of the ward to appreciate and acknowledge their professional presence as your colleague in the ministry of healing. You may thank her for taking care of your member.
5. Never dress informally when going for hospital visitation, you will embarrass the church and the profession.
6. Never talk about other illnesses similar to your client's because you may not be sure how he or she will respond to the comparison of illnesses.

7. Do not talk about someone who died in the hospital recently because of the same or different illness. This may delay healing or cause more pain.
8. Do not talk about problems at home or church in the presence of the client.
9. Never cry, even if the client is at the point of death; keep giving hope. Never be tempted to react the way the relatives will be reacting, such as sobbing.
10. Do not look hopeless in your facial expression. Put on an encouraging face full of spiritual hope.
11. Do not look shocked or unaccepting if the situation deteriorates in your presence.
12. If the patient gasps the last breath, call the sister to come and address the situation; do not touch anything, just be still. If your client dies in your presence and the relatives are present, make a little prayer of acceptance and leave. Outside the ward, continue to provide comfort and counsel with the family. Help them to make critical decisions and to share information with their relatives. Your relationship must remain professional.

TELEPHONE MINISTRY

Telephone prayers can be used by the pastor where the conditions do not allow him to go and provide a ministry of presence. It is debatable as to what extend such a prayer helps the patient. But psychologically it gives a sense of hope to the client. It is vital to know that communication here is between you, the pastor, and God. Ask God to deal with the situation without you having to go to the client. Have faith that things can happen without you being present. For some, just a call is adequate. For others it is very crucial. All pastors who are interested in this telephone ministry must remember that it can never be a substitute for the ministry of presence. Also, do not just make it a habit! Ask the person on the line if it's OK to say a little prayer. If he says fine, then you can go ahead. This is a very professional practice because the person you are talking to may be in a physical situation or surrounding that does allow for such an opportunity (or interruption). Remember, you are not praying on the phone just for the sake of it, the client must feel he needs it. Sometimes he must ask for it before you impose it on him. Others don't need it because they prefer your presence. Or, be polite; ask if it is possible for you to say a prayer. This is a pastoral, as well as a professional, matter. The person on the other side of the line might be driving or busy with another call. So, do not take it for granted that although you feel there is need for prayer at this point in time, the person you are talking to must also need it. This is not to underestimate the power and importance of prayer, but it may be suitable at another time. Know that the moment you impose a prayer on a client, it will not stick!

EQUIP THE CONGREGATION FOR PASTORAL VISITATION

The congregation must be equipped to minister to each other at any stage of the life of the congregation. Teach the church to realize the importance of caring for each other. They need one another as they must know that they are each other's keeper. A good pastor must equip leaders of the church to engage in pastoral visitation. Train the leaders and the entire church to perform this function. Reasons for this type of ministry are:

1. The congregation will learn to care for each other.
2. The process will improve their social and spiritual relationships.
3. The congregation will grow spiritually as they minister to each other.
4. The congregation will mature in their understanding of each other.
5. The church will understand the importance of the priesthood of all believers in a more pronounced manner.
6. The congregation will improve its membership drive and care.
7. The congregation will have more influence and impact in its ministry to the community.
8. The congregation will improve in its nurturing and witnessing as an evangelization method.
9. The congregation will appreciate the importance of fighting spiritual wars as one force.
10. Weaker members of the congregation are strengthened in their faith.

11. Wicked members will be assisted to change their lifestyle.
12. The congregation will learn to love one another.
13. The congregation will build on each other's spiritual confidence.
14. The church will develop a positive attitude towards each other even in the diversity of their differences as children of God. Remember, ". . . attitude can make or break you."[1]

Prayer: Almighty God, make me a good shepherd. Teach me how to care, O God. Help me to care for others the way you care for me. Amen.

1. Maxwell, *21 Indispensable Qualities of a Leader*, ii.

20

Being an Efficient Pastor

THE MEANING AND IMPORTANCE OF EFFICIENCY

CAN CHURCHES OPERATE WITHOUT pastors? The answer is debatable. In mainstream Christianity, where the issue of pastoral history of the early times emerges from the apostolic succession matters, churches cannot operate without pastors. Members of any church can preach and teach, bury or marry each other where the law allows, but they cannot administer sacraments such as baptism or Holy Communion (in some churches). The role of the pastor becomes crucial at this stage. It is the pastor's role to take care of the spiritual needs of the people of God. The pastor is trained to preach and teach the scriptures, as well as leading the church in worship. The pastor's job is to bring people to Christ together with other Christians. The pastor must do this in the most efficient way possible. The pastor must be in charge of the spiritual program of the congregation.

Most pastors in all denominations ask themselves the question, "how can I be the most efficient pastor in my church or district or conference"? It is a good thing to be the most efficient, or one of the most effective pastors, of your time in your district or church rather than being the worst or the most ineffective pastor in your church.

What does it mean to be an efficient pastor in the administration of the church? It means being able to produce expected results from the profession of pastor: to bring people to Christ and be able take care of the flock's spiritual needs, as well as their socio-economic and even political requirements as human beings. Spiritually, they must be in the right relationship with God. Economically, they must be productive citizens. This means being able to work for their own families. Politically, they must be responsible citizens. The pastor must be a role model in all these aspects of life and ministry. The question is where on earth can the church get such a pastor? He can be found somewhere in the world. The church is looking for such a pastor because it is thirsty for effective pastors: those that can deliver. A pastor who delivers is one who gets things done on time and in a correct way without unnecessary complaints. He does his work to the satisfaction of God, his conscience, and the expectation of the church or faith community of which he is given responsibility. An efficient pastor is effective in time and task management. He performs his work to the expectation of the one who oversees his work. Being an efficient pastor means being able to plan, organize, implement what has been planned on time and being able to realize expected results. Being efficient means the absence of failure in one's work. An efficient pastor avoids planning to fail in his work—he fails by planning poorly and failing to implement what has been planned. Failure to meet objectives results in being ineffective in one's pastoral work.

While the guidelines below are not in any way an exhaustive and comprehensive list, they attempt to provide you with some platform from which to start working towards excellent performance in pastoral ministry in your role as a pastor. Among other critical roles of the pastor in the congregation are the following:

1. Visioning: Where there is no vision people will perish. The pastor needs to have a vision for the congregation. The vision must be spiritually driven, although it can translate into various aspects. The vision can be short or long term. In addition, this vision must be shared with the lay leadership to begin with and then it must be taken to the entire congregation. The idea of sharing the pastor's vision is so that all members may appreciate where the church is going and coming from in terms of mission and ministry. It is not possible to achieve a vision when it is not shared by the entire congregation. Such a vision might include congregational expansion; outreach programs; fundraising, crusades; leadership needs and training; pastoral care and counseling; educational development; and many others. The pastor and the congregation must have a clear view of what must be achieved in the next five to ten years in the life of that church or congregation.

2. Preaching: Preaching is a very critical aspect of the congregation's life. This part of ministry must never be underestimated. The pas-

tor must be found to be serious with the task of preaching. The pulpit belongs to the pastor. Even if the pastor delegates someone to preach, he is still responsible for the outcome of the message preached, or lack of such results, from the message preached. It is recommended that the pastor preaches every Sunday. If this is impossible, maybe because of other ministry pressures, the pastor then must preach three of every four Sundays or four of every five Sundays in a month. Once a month, perhaps, the pulpit may be open to a layperson. In every revival the pastor must preach once or twice. He must take an active part in the spiritual life of the congregation. He must never be an observer at all. At the same time it will be embarrassing for the pastor to have a visitor take his pulpit without prior knowledge of the leadership of the church. To avoid these surprises a preaching plan must be put in place and the guests and leadership must be informed in time. Never assume they know just because you gave them a preaching plan. Check to see if they remember. If it is a lay preacher, remind the preacher about the importance of following the Christian calendar in case this might be forgotten. If it is another pastor or lay preacher taking your pulpit, find out a week before what readings or texts or message he is going to preach about. Put the information on the notice board for the people to see.

In preaching the sermon there must be a central message for the people to take home. Every sermon must answer the question: what is God saying to me and his people today? Every sermon must give people something to take home. Church is not about politics or economics or just religion or social life, although these are important. Church is about what God says to people in his word. The pastor must provide this. Church is about the good news of God through Christ. Every sermon must bring out this truth. Every sermon must move someone closer to God than they were before. The truth that saves is what people come to church for. They do not come to church to hear sociology or philosophy or psychology or any academic data, they come to hear what God is saying to them. The sermon must speak to their soul. It must speak to their situation and life experiences. It must provide a turning point in their life. So, it must be planned and well delivered. To plan a sermon means putting theological facts in order: what is God saying to his people? What must I say first and why? Where am I getting at? What do I want to achieve in the sermon? What illustrations or day-to-day stories can I use to make my theological truth more meaningful to the message I am trying to put across? What is the one central message that all people that have come to listen to me can take home today? These are some of the questions a preacher must ask when preparing to preach in any context. Preaching is one of the most taxing tasks of the pastor. A sermon can never be meaningful unless the preacher prays about it and asks God to grace it. Without prayer a sermon can just be another story. All pastors must take preaching as a central task of ministry. When people come to church they must hear a message that saves them.

3. Caring: The most fundamental task of a good pastor is to care for the faith community. You might be dynamic in your preaching—that all demons will tremble to the ground upon hearing you challenge them to come out of your members—but if you fail to care for the members, you cease to be a good shepherd. Pastoral care involves being with the flock at its weakest in life. Pastoral care is a ministry of listening and showing concern. It just comes naturally inside the pastor's work. The pastor cannot force it to happen. Either you care or you don't. It is a gift from God.

4. Time management: Poor timekeeping and management is any pastor's worst enemy. Poor time management is caused by poor planning of one's life. Never plan to be at a place when everyone else is already there. Plan to be the first at the venue for any event. Tell yourself never to be the last. Identify possible reasons why you might be late for a meeting and deal with these. All pastors who come late for meetings, or any planned event, are being managed by events instead of managing the events and activities of the church. The pastor should manage events and activities under his sphere of administration. The pastor must be on top of the situation all the time, even during crisis management. The pastor must manage time and, as the Bible says, we must make the most out of the time we have (Eph 5:16). It says that we must make the most out of every opportunity. For most effective pastors three basic steps in administration must be followed. These are: Plan, Organize, and Obey.[1] Never do what you have not planned. Clarify your vision. Follow what you have planned to do in an organized way. Match what has been planned and what is being done to achieve set goals. Being effective means doing the right things in a right way or correctly within a given schedule of time. Time management is about results.

1. White, *The Effective Pastor*, 210.

5. Evangelizing: The most critical function of the church is based on The Great Commission. Jesus told the disciples:

> All authority in heaven and on earth has been given to me. Therefore go and make disciples of all nations, baptizing them in the name of the Father and of the Son and of the Holy Spirit, and teach them to obey everything I have commanded you. And surely I am with you always, to the very end of the age (Matt 28:18–20).

To this day, this commission to evangelize is outstanding for the Christian ministry. The pastor's task is to bring people to Christ in order to conform to this commission. All other pastoral tasks are a follow-up to this great commission. The church and all congregations must spend two-thirds of the operating budget on evangelism. The pastor must have two-thirds of his working schedule on planning for this task of the church. The church must have a program of reaching out to many who have not known Christ. The Bible teaches us, "I will make you a light for the nations, that you may bring my salvation to the ends of the earth" (Isa 49:6). The pastor must remember that all work to bring people to Christ is the power of the Holy Spirit and he is an instrument to the task of evangelization.

6. Strategizing: God says, "I know the plans I have for you: plans to prosper and not to harm you, plans to give you a hope and a future" (Jer 29:11). Planning is part of God's business and we, as a church, are part of that spiritual enterprise. The work of God needs critical strategies apart from the task of preaching, praying, and caring. Some decisions on the use of available human and financial resources must be made.

We need strategic management of our church programs, and an effective pastor must be in the forefront in this process. Strategic management means the process of identifying a distinctive vision as a congregation and finding out ways through which we can realize our aspirations as a church. The purpose of strategic management in the church is to match our activities to God's call in concrete obedience in a particular context. It involves looking at the particular context of the congregation, such as the unique history of the congregation, gifts, catchment area of the membership, and the network of relationships and ministry.

An effective pastor makes sure that planned meetings are held and objectives followed up within given periods of time. Tasks must be given during such meetings and certain persons are tasked to follow up on goals set and report back as scheduled. The effective pastor must be very good at following up on set tasks. This is the stage where a distinction can be made between an effective pastor and a non-effective one.

7. Servant leadership: The purpose of having a pastor as a leader of the congregation is to provide three functions: doctrinal, juridical, and legislative.[2] Doctrine means teaching. The pastor must teach church doctrine. This means he must spell out clearly what the church believes and be able to explain why. This is the function of an effective pastor. Be knowledgeable about the doctrines of the church.

Jurisdiction, centers on the moral discipline of the church. Whether we like it or not, there will always be issues of moral discipline in the church. It is the role of the pastor to administer this function on behalf of the church. For the sake of order the pastor must see to it that the discipline of the church is soundly administered.

Legislation centers on the proper conduct of worship in relation to the maintenance of order in the church. It is vital that the order of worship be administered in a way that continues to uplift the lives of the church community. How do we establish a new faith community? Who will provide spiritual leadership on the new congregation? Who performs the sacraments of baptism or the Lord's Supper? What determines the number of bishops or pastors? This is what legislation in the church provides. The effective pastor must be in a position to spell out the orderly way things ought to be in the given legislation. In most cases, there is a constitution of the church, which provides such legislation.

Other functions of effective pastoral leadership are: leading in worship; offering pastoral prayers; preaching the word; administering the sacraments; preserving the doctrine of the gospel; labor for conversions; comforting the tempted and weary; suffering with those who suffer; caring for the poor and visiting the sick; and conducting the life of the church including meetings and order.

8. Encouraging fellowship:[3] One of the vital tasks an effective pastor must handle with care is the issue of unity in the church or congregation. This can be checked by finding out how close the general membership is to each other. Experience has shown that every congregation has some members who hate each other for personal reasons. The pastor must en-

2. Ibid., 169.

3. Anderson, *Effective Pastor*, 336.

courage fellowship for all the members of the congregation. The Greek word *koininia,* which means association, communion, fellowship, close relationship, helps us to unite the congregation in the name of the Lord for the good of the church. When the church or congregation is united it works better and more effectively.

9. Ministry of presence at special events: An effective pastor must be seen at any member's special event including weddings, funerals, graduation, and maybe commissioning to higher office. This is in relation to the personal life of the membership of the church and congregation. But in terms of professional presence an effective pastor must never miss, for any reason, such events as Christmas, Easter,[4] New Year's Eve, annual retreat, and harvest thanksgiving. Ordinarily, the pastor must preach the first Sunday of the year and the last Sunday of the year. The Christmas sermon of the year must come from the pastor. He may delegate but most congregations prefer the pastor to preach on special occasions of the Christian calendar.

BIBLICAL TASKS OF AN EFFECTIVE PASTOR

1. Equipping: The pastor must equip the saints for the work of ministry by teaching them how to preach, witness, care for one another, and to teach each other about God and Christian ministry.
2. Shepherding: In the word of God, (1 Pet 5:2), it is a pastor's function to shepherd the flock. This must be extended to the congregation to care for one another. The term pastor means shepherd and carries clear connotation for looking after the flock. Christian witness extends from the pastorate, if it is highly organized.
3. Leading by example: Leading means guiding, showing the way, or giving direction. The congregation must not lead itself. It must rely heavily on the pastor's direction and guidance.
4. Preaching: In any church the pulpit belongs to the pastor. All other preachers of the same pulpit must be invited by the pastor.
5. Teaching: Teaching is a critical ministry of the pastor. Two-thirds of the sermons preached by Jesus were teaching sermons. This ministry must never be underestimated. An effective pastor must create space for the teaching of the word of God within the congre-

4. Ibid., 206–7.

gation. Teach the church in small groups or in the time for worship service. Teach the church the word of God and how humankind relies on God for its life and sustenance.

6. Correcting: The pastor must correct problems the church and world are facing in a loving way. A lot of care must be taken not to correct personal conflicts and grudges in the sermon. We do not preach hate, but love. We do not preach people, but Jesus as good news. The pastor must correct wrong with love and care.

Prayer: Lord Jesus, make me a role model of love and care. Teach me how to correct wrong with rightness, rebuke sin with a sense of patience and love. Amen.

21

Leadership Styles in Ministry

MEANING OF LEADERSHIP STYLE

LEADERSHIP STYLE IN MINISTRY refers to the way a pastor decides to lead his congregation. Style could mean method or type or pattern. For example, certain pastors prefer meeting their leaders once a month to review congregational developments or progress on set objectives. Others prefer giving the congregation monthly financial reports through the finance committee as a way of motivating the congregation to give generously to the church. Some pastors just share their vision with the leadership and then delegates responsibilities to subcommittees. All these are styles of leadership that work well in various contexts. There is no one best style for all congregations. Neither is there a perfect style.

Before discussing leadership styles it is prudent to define Old Testament and New Testament principles of leadership or administration. Biblical leadership takes place when divinely appointed men and women respond in obedience to God's call to the ministry.[1] In addition they recognize the importance of preparation time, allowing the Holy Spirit to develop their tenderness of heart and skill of hands. They carry out their ministry with a deep conviction of God's will and an acute awareness of the contemporary issues they and their followers face. The success of a congregation depends mostly on the leadership style of the pastor and the lay leadership of that particular church. The congregation has no problem following the style of leadership given to it by the pastor and those who work with him or her. If he or she misleads them, they will pick it up in no time. Sometimes this lack of leadership will become the source of many problems to follow. Such problems may in-

1. Berkley, *Leadership Handbook*, 147.

clude mistrust or lack of confidence in the pastor by the lay leadership or vice versa. The following, in general, appears to be the Old Testament principles of leadership:

IN THE OLD TESTAMENT

1. Biblical administration begins by divine appointment: This is what became of Noah, Abraham, Moses, and Aaron. They were obedient, humble, and honest. Joshua, David, and Nehemiah were also among some of the best leaders in Israel's history of liberation.
2. Leadership requires accountability: The law spelled out the greater responsibilities of those appointed (Lev 4:22). Moses hit the rock in anger and was forbidden entry into Canaan. Miriam criticized Moses and became leprous.
3. Leadership requires time for preparation: Joshua served for years as Moses' servant. David was a soldier before his anointing. The life of Nehemiah appears to be same in terms of a lengthy preparation.
4. Leadership requires skill: Nehemiah provides an example of one who could organize, plan, delegate, supervise, arbitrate, recruit, train, and evaluate.
5. Leadership requires a heart sensitive to spiritual things: David was a skilled fighter and God selected him because of his heart (1 Sam 16:7).

IN THE NEW TESTAMENT

1. Leadership is servanthood: Christ bears this example. So does Paul and the other apostles and elders.
2. Leadership is stewardship: We see in the New Testament the leaders being given the task of looking after others and God's treasure.
3. Leadership is shared power: We must share pastoral responsibility (Phil 2:4).
4. Leadership is ministry: Selfishness is not allowed. The emphasis of *diakonia* is vital (Rom 12:8).
5. Leadership is providing a model of behavior: The Paul–Timothy relationship teaches us this (1 Tim 4:11–16, 2 Tim 3:10–15).

6. Leadership is membership in the Body: A good leader must identify with the membership of the church without discriminating against any. We see this also is Romans 12:4–5.

Any pastor who needs to create a good pastoral relationship with the congregation must always remember these Biblical principles of leadership because they do shape one's pastoral etiquette.

ADDITIONAL STYLES OF LEADERSHIP

To be an effective pastor the following leadership styles are recommended,[2] among many others:

1. Visionary leadership style: To be an effective administrator one must be visionary. This means you must have a vision of what you want the church or organization to achieve within a given period. To achieve your vision you may need to form teams that will help you realize your goals or vision. The teams must be managed through progress reports that must focus on the set objectives. Keep asking yourself the question: What is my vision here? Then what is the vision of this congregation? It is not enough just to have a vision. The vision must be shared with the leadership of the congregation. Effective communication of the vision to a congregation relies on the credibility of the pastor's vision.[3] Do the people believe in it? Can they believe it? Any mission's vision must have credibility if people are to commit themselves to it. The vision may be to increase membership in the next two or so years, and how must this be achieved? The congregation will help you realize this goal through set programs and people. These must be checked from set times. There must be persons and times set to check progress. You as the leader must do this. Most poor leaders delegate and fail to get down to the targets they have set. Attend all committee meetings you have set. Do not rely on leaders of those committees no matter how good they may be.

2. Directional leadership style: A very good leader must show the church which direction to go. Every leader worth his or her title must make a difference. Know your weakness and avoid repeating it to avoid being foolish as a public figure. If you know you are emotional, for example, and you are short-tempered avoid responding to provocative

2. Hybels, *Courageous Leadership*, 141.

3. Ibid.

statements. People may provoke you to test your spiritual maturity. Be moderate. Focus on issues that matter. Move forward instead of following swayed attention. Direct the church to its main focus. It is a sign of weak leadership style to respond to an unclear statement from the floor, for instance, if you are chairing a meeting. When you are not sure of how to handle most difficult situations consult one or two individuals you consider to be very constructive to your work. After their advice take time to think through what they have said and then move forward as reasonably as possible.

3. Strategic leadership style: This involves putting plans into action one step after the other, according to the priorities as viewed by the leadership. The steps must be appropriate: well timed, well placed, well intentioned, and well managed. Wrong personnel abort well-intentioned plans. Avoid using them to achieve your goals. Yes-men are no good either. Find those who are positively critical of your work and take them to task to tell you what they think you need to achieve. All your strategies to achieve God's work must be built on good will, reasonableness, and critical reflection of what must be achieved within a given period of time. Never do everything at once. Never aim to please those who hate you or talk bad of you. Aim to please God within a free framework of mind; in turn, everyone will appreciate your work. Know what you want to achieve and take smaller, but meaningful, steps to achieve it.

4. Managing leadership style: This involves the ability to organize people, processes, and resources to achieve a mission. A good manager brings order out of chaos. He or she motivates the team by establishing progress markers at appropriate stages of any process. This leadership style calls for more action than just rhetoric. Good examples of such managing leaders in the Bible include Nehemiah, Joseph, and Moses.

5. Motivational leadership style: Jesus motivated the disciples the way he trained them. He tells them, "I am with you always" and, indeed, he was. This motivated them. Motivational leaders do not get bitter or vengeful when morale sinks. They view it as an opportunity to dream of new ways to inspire and lift the spirits of everyone on the team. The Lord often motivated his audience through a reward in heaven. He planned retreats for his staff. He changed Simon's name and honored him as Peter, on which the church would be built. He gave him the title rock, a sign of strength. He sent his disciples two by two and provided feedback

time. At one point he tells them you are my friends if you do what I command you. At another stage he tells them abide in me and I in you. The pastor must always motivate the congregation to work hard by showing confidence in what they do, recognize their efforts, take them out for retreats, create special occasions for them to be on their own. They will be motivated to do God's work in a special way.

6. Shepherding style of leadership: This involves drawing people together regardless of their ages, race, and gender and building a team out of them for the purpose of doing God's work. This involves developing a passion for them in terms of loving them, nurturing them, supporting consistently them, listening to them patiently, and praying for them. King David was such a leader (2 Sam 23). The pastor must respect whatever people bring to the church in terms of service, presence, prayers, or anything they consider valuable.

7. Team-building leadership style: This involves team-building in the work of the church. A good soccer team is one that works neatly as a team to create a winning spirit before the actual winning. The pastor must create the right people with the right abilities and the right character. Proper combinations make it possible for things to happen the expected way.

8. Bridge-building style of leadership: This involves the diplomatic style of leadership, especially in circumstances where the church seems to be facing serious divisions. Bridge-builders love the challenge of mixing with people of diverse opinions and cultures and relates to them without much difficulty, if any. A good pastor must not be rigid in terms of focus, relations, and tradition. Be positively flexible.

SOME HIGH-IMPACT LEADERSHIP STYLES

a) Identify your own leadership style.
b) Determine if your style fits your current leadership situation.
c) Identify the leadership style of each member of your team.
d) Match each leadership need with leadership gaps on your team.
e) Commit yourself to developing strong leadership styles and identify weaknesses, as well.

TEAMWORK[4]

Qualities of effective teamwork leadership:

a) Clear vision
b) Correct use of power
c) Accountability
d) Mutual trust
e) Willingness to delegate

SKILLS OF TEAM LEADERSHIP

a) Effective communication
b) Motivation
c) Proper team choice
d) Goal setting
e) Delegation
f) Decision making

Prayer: Father, teach me your style of leading the church. Correct my physical intelligence to suit your spiritual guidelines. Transform my framework of mind. Give me a sense of accountability for my actions. Amen.

4. Chalke and Relph, *Making a Team Work*, 55.

22

Self-Evaluation

In any organization such as the church, self-evaluation of work is important. Do not be afraid of being evaluated or evaluating your own work. Evaluation helps us as the church to see areas that need to be improved. Being scared of evaluation is a sign of weak leadership. A good leader must know and appreciate his strengths and weaknesses, and learn from both to develop opportunities for growth in one's work. Challengers must never destroy a leader; instead, they must be sources of new energy for excellence in performance. Below are some tools that can be used by the pastor to evaluate God's work in the ministry of administration.

GENERAL SIGNS OF EFFECTIVE ADMINISTRATION

1. Significant growth in membership
2. Unnecessary postponement of programs
3. Visible development of infrastructure
4. Meaningful professional connections with colleagues
5. Relative absence of conflict and tension
6. Meeting deadlines for all programs
7. Realization of set goals as scheduled
8. Timely evaluation of programs
9. Earning confidence of the people
10. Creating a sense of independent thinking and perception
11. Evaluation of a spiritual relationship with God
12. Prompt response to communication

CRITICAL PITFALLS TO AVOID IN ADMINISTRATION

1. Splitting the organization or church due to personal conflicts and personality differences
2 Paying more attention to one group of people at the expense of others
3. Taking sides with one group in times of conflict
4. Taking too long to attend to challenges and problems
5. Labeling or giving names to your critics or difficult church members
6. Borrowing money or items from subordinates or church members
7. Self-pitying to earn the attention of members or the leadership or subordinates
8. Doubting
9. Excessive hunger for power
10. Dishonesty
11. Losing temper
12. Ignoring your conscience
13. Dictating decisions where dialogue and democratic processes are required
14. Taking personal issues to the pulpit or into church business
15. Coming late for some or all activities of the church
16. Being absent without giving a meaningful excuse
17. Losing focus
18. Losing patience
19. Taking shortcuts in solving problems
20. Lacking respect for other people
21. Despising other people
22. Embarrassing other people in public

SIGNS OF POSITIVE RELATIONS IN THE CONGREGATION

1. Minimum or no social and spiritual tension among the members
2. Attendance figures at worship services show an upward trend
3. The level of giving shows an upward movement
4. Attendance at church meetings show a consistent trend of participation by all those involved
5. The level of participation by leaders during such meetings and worship services show active growth

6. Punctuality at meetings, revivals, crusades show significant commitment
7. The members do not hesitate to take positions of leadership
8. The leaders of the church do not fear being evaluated by anyone
9. Nomination and election on leaders' day is not found to be tense

SUMMARY OF EFFECTIVE METHODS OF CHURCH MANAGEMENT

Some people have identified with the autocratic style of administering their organizations. The leader dictates the pace and the way things should be done. The leader does not give administrative space to the followers so that they may have a say in the running of the organization. There is minimal contact between the leader and the subordinates. Followers have to follow the policies and procedures as laid down in the code of conduct or constitution. Others have found the participative style to be effective. This style allows a lot of interaction and democracy through group discussion, involvement, consensus, and second-opinion checks between the leader and the people being led.

Yet still others find effective the laissez-faire style of leadership where the leadership does not seem to care much about the way things go. This type of administration does not seem to care about whether things go wrong or not, as long as the organization exists and they get paid, that is fine. It takes things lightly.

In the context of the church, the following universally effective, and key, styles can make administration or leadership in the church most effective:[1]

1. Spiritual focus: God is the origin and destination of life, and through prayer, Bible study, and worship we hope to realize eternal life. Anchor your administration, management, leadership, business, and success on God.

2. Enthusiasm: Very good ideas presented in a dull, listless, and uninteresting manner may seem irrelevant. The same ideas communicated with enthusiasm can light the fire of commitment that leads to positive change.

1. Miller, *Leadership is the Key*, 113.

3. Joyful attitude: A joyful spirit draws followers to a leader's goals as it creates a sense of humor; attracts a sense of relaxation in followers, which helps them enjoy their work; and shows an indication that a leader values followers. All these can influence creativity and quality in people's work. A joyful attitude produces positive results.
4. Hope: A powerful administrator must always have a sense of hope that what is being done can bring meaning and positive change to people's lives. Without hope and faith not much can be achieved in life.
5. High energy level: The work of the church involves working long hours most times with little, if any, meaningful remuneration or little appreciation. Several demands come at the same time and the pastor must have the stamina to deal effectively with such demands.
6. Self-discipline: This helps the pastor to supercharge for greater spiritual and professional achievement. It also assists the pastor to attend to critical issues with a sense of maturity, integrity, and confidence.
7. Positive appearance: Neat clothing and hair do not bring people into the kingdom of God but if the package is shabby, people will not bother with its contents. They will not have time to examine the contents. Positive appearance enhances the pastor's message.
8. Tactfulness: Every leader must be tactful in dealing with administrative issues in the congregation. Do not take things for granted. It is important to know the difference between what can be said and what should be said. You can avoid saying things that may, in fact, bring more harm than the intended good. Train your tongue to limit unnecessary sayings that in the future are quoted in the negative.
9. Flexibility: A good administrator must have an open mind to accept other people's ideas and have time alone to examine the pros and cons of each of the new ideas. Do not just reject or accept things without being critical to them.
10. Conviction: It is not possible to achieve a goal if the administrator has no conviction that what is to be achieved can make it through difficult circumstances.

PERSONAL EVALUATION QUESTIONNAIRE IN MINISTRY

Every good spiritual pastor must have a well-set and clear method through which people working with him should evaluate his work. The following may be used as a general format for personal evaluation for one's effectiveness in the ministry of administration of the congregation or any other setting. The pastor can use this instrument once a year for self-evaluation. All members or top leaders can fill it in without writing their names on it. It is a very helpful instrument to improve one's work.

Instructions: Please put a tick where appropriate: Each category carries 10 points as follows: Excellent = 5, Very Good = 3, Good = 2, Poor = 0

1. Preaching:
   ______ Excellent
   ______ Very good
   ______ Good
   ______ Poor
2. Are sermons spiritually uplifting?
   ______ Excellent
   ______ Very good
   ______ Good
   ______ Poor
3. Pastoral visitation:
   ______ Excellent
   ______ Very good
   ______ Good
   ______ Poor
4. Teaching the Bible:
   ______ Excellent
   ______ Very good
   ______ Good
   ______ Poor
5. Organization and administration of meetings:
   ______ Excellent
   ______ Very good
   ______ Good
   ______ Poor

6. Ability to solve issues and problems on time:
   ______ Excellent
   ______ Very good
   ______ Good
   ______ Poor
7. Management of funerals and weddings:
   ______ Excellent
   ______ Very good
   ______ Good
   ______ Poor
8. Time management: punctuality:
   ______ Excellent
   ______ Very good
   ______ Good
   ______ Poor
9. Dressing and neatness:
   ______ Excellent
   ______ Very good
   ______ Good
   ______ Poor
10. Self-confidence:
   ______ Excellent
   ______ Very good
   ______ Good
   ______ Poor
11. Ability to handle conflict effectively:
   ______ Excellent
   ______ Very good
   ______ Good
   ______ Poor
12. Accepts criticism:
   ______ Excellent
   ______ Very good
   ______ Good
   ______ Poor

13. Leads worship well:
    ______ Excellent
    ______ Very good
    ______ Good
    ______ Poor

14. Motivates giving for the church:
    ______ Excellent
    ______ Very good
    ______ Good
    ______ Poor

15. Motivates evangelism:
    ______ Excellent
    ______ Very good
    ______ Good
    ______ Poor

16. Honesty:
    ______ Excellent
    ______ Very good
    ______ Good
    ______ Poor

17. Attentive to children's spiritual needs including short sermons for them:
    ______ Excellent
    ______ Very good
    ______ Good
    ______ Poor

18. Communicates clearly and effectively:
    ______ Excellent
    ______ Very good
    ______ Good
    ______ Poor

19. Training and equipping of leaders:
    ______ Excellent
    ______ Very good
    ______ Good
    ______ Poor

20. Delegates responsibility well:
    ______ Excellent
    ______ Very good
    ______ Good
    ______ Poor

Prayer: God, please evaluate my work and rebuke me where I am going wrong. Praise me where I have done well. Inspire me for excellence. Visit my conscience. Make me your friend, even though I am your child. Amen.

23

Conclusion

An attempt has been made in this book to show that it is possible to administer the church where various problems exist provided that the pastor is conscious of the fact that God is in charge and in control of every situation. Success is a gift from God. We must all pray for this gift. We must never be discouraged in God's work because he works through us. If we succeed in God's work, then that success belongs to God. Administering the church is God's business; the pastor is just an instrument. At the end of it all glory must be given to God.

Critical problems in the life of the church or community must not deter the leaders of the church from being good stewards. Problems in the church and country are like a storm. They come and go. Even if they were to stay with us, the strength to overcome them comes from the Lord who in his own power managed to walk above them, in them, through them, and out of them. So can we. The Apostle Paul comforts church leaders when he writes to the church in Philippi to say, ". . . I can do all things through Christ who gives me strength" (Phil 4:13). The strength and willpower comes from God. We must not tell God how big our problems are but, rather, tell our problems how big our God is. It is true that God is unique, unlike other gods, so he deals with our challenges in the church and in the community in a special way.

All the chapters in this book are pieced together to show that church administration cannot be taken for granted. It is very difficult to lead the church if the pastor does not seek guidance from the Holy Spirit. At the same time the pastor cannot call other people to Christ if he doubts the power of the Holy Spirit as a source of strength and force that changes lives. We must all walk a tight rope with and in Christ to lead the church with a sense of passion for salvation. Without a passion for the ministry that leads to eternal life no pastor can manage to provide a service of quality administration to the church. At the same time it is impossible to be a successful leader in the church when one has no personal relationship with God. Every pastor needs to realize a child–parent relationship with God (1 Pet 1:14). This relationship helps the pastor to motivate other Christians to do greater things for the Lord.

The pastor must be a tither and one who gives to the Lord generously. The pastor must be an example of one who gives cheerfully. The lesson here is simple: if you give your best, and cheerfully, you will be rewarded most abundantly. In addition, giving to the Lord is a way of worshipping God and fighting personal poverty. The challenge of poverty is fought through cheerful giving to the Lord. There are spiritual battles to be won, critical decisions to be made, some hard planning to be done, some pride or criticism to be managed, some popularity to be lost (or won), some love (or hatred) to be experienced and, most importantly, some tremendous work of God to be achieved in a given period of time. These can only be won by an added closeness to the Lord. No compromise! But, the pastor as a teacher, administrator, prophet, apostle, preacher, shepherd, and counselor must be on top of the situation as a spiritual person. However, the pastor does not walk this spiritual journey alone, but together with God every step of the way. The steps might be steep and slippery, but the journey is safe for we all know that those who wait upon the Lord shall be given new strength; they shall run and not be weary; and they shall walk, and not faint (Isa 40:31).

When you face problems in the congregation, in faith God will be close by to help you out provided you match your spiritual battles with your spiritual commitment. This balance is important for a successful ministry to be achieved. If you are an honest and positively firm pastor, you are likely to lose friends and popular members of your congregation. Listen to the Holy Spirit rather than simply those who seek your attention and do very little, if anything, for the Lord.

God continues to work wonders for us all, helping us sail through troubled times. In God we trust. In God we have the strength to overcome all transgressions. In God we see the vision for success in all our work. In God we have the power to grow spiritually and evaluate our faith and our work. We learn and teach all church leaders in our congregations to see challenges and problems the way Christ would look at them. This inspires hope, trust, obedience, faith, and a future full of hope. God motivates us to see problems as sources of courage and inspiration; burdens as everlasting tunnels of blessing; and uncertainties or ambiguities as sources of faith.

> *Prayer*: Dear God, give me the strength to pray even when I am weary. Help me to remember what Paul says: "And we know that God causes everything to work together for the good of those who love God and are called according to his purpose for them" (Rom 8:28). Amen.

Epilogue

I have watched over 100,000 families over years of investment counseling. I always saw greater prosperity and happiness among those families who tithed than those who didn't.

—Sir John Templeton

Failure is the opportunity to begin again, this time more intelligently.

—Henry Ford

Everything that irritates us about others can lead us to an understanding of ourselves.

—Carl Jung

Anyone who has never made a mistake has never tried anything new.

—Albert Einstein

Be like a postage stamp. Stick to one thing until you get there.

—Josh Billings

Nothing in life is to be feared, it is only to be understood.

—Marie Curie

A joyful heart is the inevitable result of a heart burning with love.

—Mother Teresa

Success is not the key to happiness. If you love what you are doing, you will be successful.

—Albert Schweitzer

Sensible people control their temper; they earn their respect by overlooking wrongs.

Proverbs 19:11

. . . money is a barometer of your spirituality, because the way you handle your money is an indication of your performance as a Christian steward.

—John F. MacArthur Jr., Author

The silver is mine, and the gold is mine,
says the Lord Almighty.

Haggai 2:8

Scarcity is a problem for everyone. Each individual must deal with the problem because it is a condition of human existence.

—R. K. Klay, Author

I judge all things by the price they shall gain in eternity.

—John Wesley, Founder of Methodism

All our difficulties are only platforms for the manifestation of God's grace, power and love.

—Hudson Taylor

Choose associations with people who focus on your future not on your past.

—Paula White, Author

Bibliography

Adams, J. E. *Christian Counselor's Manual.* New Jersey: Presbyterian & Reformed Publishing Co., 1973.

Anderson, R. C. *The Effective Pastor: A Practical Guide to the Ministry*. Chicago: Moody, 1985.

Atkinson, R. L., et al. *Introduction to Psychology*. San Diego, FL: HBJ, 1990.

Benton, J. *Gender Questions: Biblical Manhood and Womanhood in the Contemporary World.* Auburn: Sovereign World, 2000.

Berkley, J. D. *Leadership Handbook of Management and Administration*. Grand Rapids: Baker, 1994.

Book of Discipline. *The United Methodist Church.* Nashville: Abingdon, 2004.

Brown, R. *Surviving the Loss of a Loved One: Living Through Grief.* UK: Autumn House, 1999.

Carter, D. *10 Smart Things Women Can Do to Build a Better Life.* Eugene, OR: Harvest House, 2006.

Chalke, S., and P. Relph. *Making a Team Work: How to Lead a Team Effectively.* Eastburne, UK: Kingsway, 1995.

Chaplin, J. P. *Dictionary of Psychology*. New York: Dell, 1975.

Chivaura, A. "Stress." Unpublished paper, presented at the Health and Safety Workshop, Harare, ZW, n.d.

Chiza, B. *The Blessing Connector: Your Gateway To Worship Through Giving.* Zimbabwe: Yorik (Pvt) Ltd., 2006.

Clinebell, H. J. *Basic Types of Pastoral Counseling.* Nashville: Abingdon, 1966.

Cole, E., and N. Cole. *The Unique Woman-Insight and Wisdom to Maximize your Life.* Tulsa, OK, 1989.

Collins, G. R. *Christian Counseling: A Comprehensive Guide.* Nashville: Thomas Nelson, 2007.

———. ed. *Counseling and the Search for Meaning.* Dallas: Word, 1987.

Douglas, J. D., ed. *The New International Dictionary of the Christian Church.* Exeter, UK: The Paternoster, 1978.

Dube, M. W., ed. *Africa Praying: A Handbook on HIV/AIDS Sensitive Sermon Guidelines and Liturgy.* Geneva: WCC, 2004.

———. ed. *HIV/AIDS and the Curriculum: Methods of Integrating HIV/AIDS in Theological Programmes.* Geneva: WCC, 2004.

Facing AIDS. *The Challenge, the Churches' Response: A WCC Study Document.* Geneva: WCC Publications, 2004.

Farris, L. W. *Ten Commandments for Pastors Leaving a Congregation.* Grand Rapids, MI: W. B. Eerdmans, 2006.

Gordon, B. *The Foundations of Christian Living: A Practical Guide to Christian Growth.* Chichester, UK: Sovereign World, 1988.

Hull, B. *The Disciple-Making Pastor.* Grand Rapids, MI: Revell, 1988.

Hybels, B. *Courageous Leadership*. Grand Rapids, MI: Zondervan, 2002.

Jefkins, F. *Public Relations.* London: Pitman, 1980.

Kendall, R. T. *The Gift of Giving.* London: Hodder & Stoughton, 1982.

———. *Tithing: a Call to Serious Biblical Giving.* Michigan: Zondervan, 1982.

Lawrence, M. *The Dynamics of Spiritual Formation.* Grand Rapids, MI: Baker, 2000.

Lindgren, A. *Foundations for Purposeful Church Administration.* Nashville: Abingdon, 1965.

Logan, R. E., and L. Short. *Mobilizing for Compassion: Moving People into Ministry.* Grand Rapids, MI: Revell, 1994.

Lunn, M. *Treasures in Heaven: The abundant life of stewardship*. Kansas City: Nazarene Publishing, 1963.

MacArthur, J. F. *God's Plan for Giving.* Chicago: Moody, 1982.

Marshall, T. *Understanding Leadership: Fresh Perspectives on the Essentials of New Testament Leadership.* Tonbridge, UK: Sovereign World, 1991.

Maxwell, J. C. *The 4 Pillars of Leadership.* Cape Town, RSA: Struik Christian, 2003.

———. *The 21 Indispensable Qualities of a Leader: Becoming the Person Others Will Want to Follow.* Nashville: Thomas Nelson, 1999.

McDowell, J. *Building Your Self-Image.* Wheaton, IL: Living Books, 1984.

Mhlanga, S. *Christian Aids Task Force Manual.* 2008.

Miller, H. *Leadership is the Key: Unlocking Your Ministry Effectiveness.* Nashville: Abingdon, 1997.

Munroe, M. *Understanding the Purpose and Power of Woman.* PA: Whitaker House, 2001.

One Body Vol. 1. *North–South Reflections in the Face of HIV and AIDS.* Nordic-Foccisa Church Cooperation, n.d.

One Body Vol. 2. *AIDS and the Worshipping Community.* Nordic-Foccisa Church Cooperation, n.d.

Pettit, P., ed. *Foundations of Spiritual Formation: A Community Approach to Becoming Like Christ.* Grand Rapids, MI: Kregel, 2008.

Powers, B. P., ed. *Church Administration Handbook.* Nashville: Broadman, 1985.

Sanders, J. O. *Spiritual Leadership.* Chicago: Moody, 1977.

Sues, L. J. C. *A New Pentecost?* New York: Seabury, 1994.

WCC. *"A WCC Study Document" on Facing AIDS, the Challenge: The Church's Response,* 1997. http://www.wcc-coe.org.

Tozer, A. W. *The Counselor Straight Talk about the Holy Spirit from a 20th Century Prophet.* Pennsylvania: Christian Publications, 1993.

Turner, J. J. *Christian Leadership Handbook.* Los Angeles: Howard, 1982.

White, E. G. *Steps to Christ, Southern Publishing Association.* RSA: Kennelworth, n.d.

White, P. *The Effective Pastor: Christian Leadership for the Twenty-first Century.* Fearn, UK: Christian Focus, 1998.

Wilson, E. *Stress proof your life: 52 brilliant ideas for taking control.* Oxford: infinite ideas, n.d.

Zenger, J., and J. Folkman. *The Handbook for Leaders: 24 Lessons for Extraordinary Leadership.* Berkshire, UK: McGraw-Hill, 2007.

Lightning Source UK Ltd.
Milton Keynes UK
UKHW021336050819
347427UK00011B/2501/P